Jim Crawford

Treasury of Basketball Drills

from Top Coaches

Treasury of Basketball Drills

from Top Coaches

Compiled and Edited by

JACK RICHARDS

PARKER PUBLISHING COMPANY, INC. ● West Nyack, N.Y.

LIBRARY OF CONGRESS
CATALOG CARD NUMBER: 79–126811

PRINTED IN THE UNITED STATES OF AMERICA
ISBN–0-13–930438–X
BC

DEDICATION

To My Mother and Father

and

To the Coaches Who
Made This Book Possible

Introduction

For some time I have made a habit of exchanging ideas regarding practice drills with coaches whom I've met at basketball clinics. It occurred to me that a book presenting the *favorite* practice drill of some of our country's leading basketball coaches would be an extremely valuable aid to other coaches on all levels of competition. While a number of basketball drill books have been produced, none provide an opportunity for individual coaches to present their own favorite drills.

The range of coaching levels included in the book extends from high school to professional basketball and includes some of the finest names in the coaching ranks. The book represents over 2200 years of coaching experience. The coaches have won over 33,000 games and have produced over 1350 championships. Included in this list are several NCAA Champions, NIT winners, National Junior College Champions, and High School State Champions.

It is my sincere hope that all coaches will find something of value within the covers of this book.

Jack Richards

ACKNOWLEDGMENTS

The credit for this book must go to the great coaches who contributed unselfishly of their time and talents. I consider it a privilege to have been associated with them in this effort and I sincerely hope the book may add something to the game of basketball.

I owe special thanks to Mrs. Adeline Polito and her secretarial training class for handling the correspondence.

To my wife, Linda, who has continued to provide me with understanding and encouragement, I extend my grateful appreciation.

Contents

5

Treasury of Basketball Drills

from Top Coaches

1

Shooting Drills

Shooting is probably the most attractive part of the game of basketball. Players practice the skill for long periods of time without being prodded by the coach. It is an activity from which they derive enjoyment during the off-season or even after a hard practice session is concluded. As a result, coupled with better techniques of instruction, shooting percentages have steadily climbed during the years. Basketball players are better shooters today, and they will continue to improve each year because shooting is a skill that can be learned. Coaches everywhere have devised excellent methods of instructing their players in this all-important area, and the results have been extremely rewarding.

Floyd Brown

North Carolina College at Durham

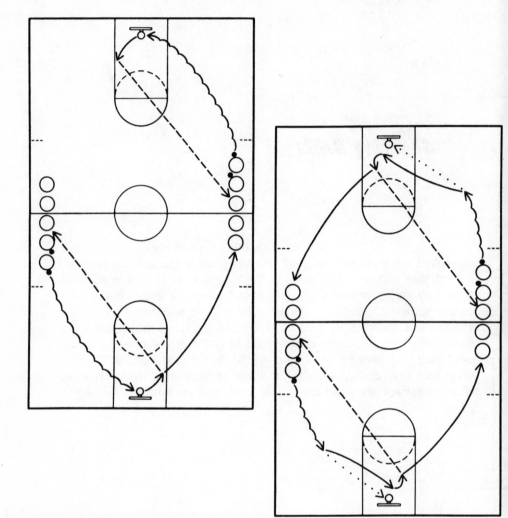

DIAGRAM 1. This is a straight line layup shot drill. Two balls are used in each line. After retrieving the ball and passing it back to the line he came from, the player goes to the end of the line at the other end of the court.

DIAGRAM 2. In this drill the player dribbles, stops, and shoots a jump shot. After getting the ball he goes to the other line.

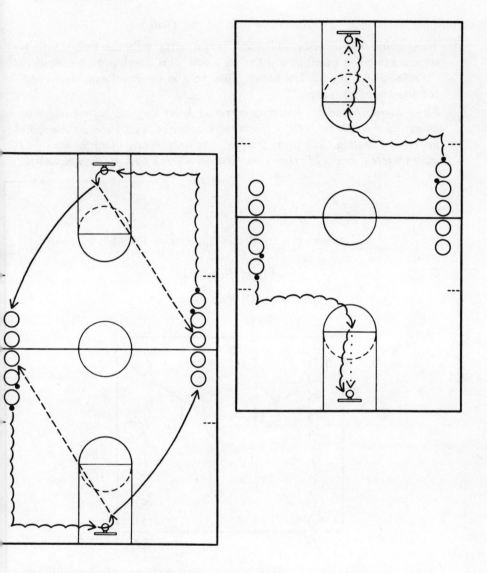

DIAGRAM 3. The player dribbles to the corner, cuts sharply to the basket down the baseline for the shot.

DIAGRAM 4. The player dribble cuts to center court to the top of the circle or free throw line for a jump shot or he fakes a stop for a shot and drives in for a layup.

All of these drill patterns will allow the player to work on his special fakes while having the ball. These drills are reversed to be run from the left-hand side of the court.

Special Value of the Drill

These drills help develop individual player skills with the ball. There is some rebounding possible and the pass out helps develop pass release to the release spot for the fast break. They help in the development of even-handedness of all players.

Floyd Brown began his coaching career at West Virginia State College as an assistant coach in 1949. After three seasons at West Virginia, he came to North Carolina College at Durham. As head coach there he won 243 games while losing 173. His teams also won three CIAA Championships.

DRIBBLE AND PIVOT SHOOTING DRILL

Floyd Burdette

University of Tennessee at Martin

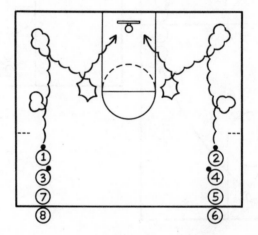

1. **Four balls are used in this drill with O2, O4, O1 and O3 having a ball.**
2. **The dribbler on the right side uses his right hand, and on the reverse pivot at the top of the circle and in the corner we change hands on the dribble for protection. From the corner pivot the left hand is used, and on the reverse pivot at the free throw line a change of hands occurs again to protect the ball.**
3. **The jump, crip, or under and up shot is taken in this drill.**
4. **The reverse of this is used by the players on the left side.**

5. **The movement on this drill occurs when O2 gets to the second pivot; O1 will start and when O1 gets to his second pivot, O4 starts his dribble. This keeps four players in motion at the same time.**
6. **After this drill is learned, it must be run at full speed.**

Special Value of the Drill

1. Players learn to dribble and protect the ball.
2. Players learn to pivot and change hands while protecting the ball.
3. It helps develop body balance and control while handling the ball.
4. Provides practice on three different shots within the 15-foot area.

Floyd Burdette began coaching in 1945 and has been at the University of Tennessee at Martin since 1951. During this time his teams have won 271 games while losing 223. During the seasons of 1965–66 and 1966–67, the Vols won the Western Division Championship of the VSAC. Burdette's recent honors include selection to the Hall of Fame at Murray State University.

FULL COURT LAYUPS

Dick Campbell

The Citadel

1. **On whistle, X1 and X4 drive for layups.**
2. **X5 follows for X1 and X12 follows for X4.**
3. **X5 then hands to X2 for layup and X12 hands to X3 for layup.**
4. **After X1 shoots, he will get behind X9 and X4 will get behind X8.**
5. **X5 will shoot behind X3 and X12 will shoot behind X2.**
6. **Once the drill is started there will be continuous movement.**

Special Value of the Drill

1. Continuous movement (ideal when eight men are used).
2. Good conditioning drill which involves shooting.
3. Once drill is started it does not require supervision.
4. Develops good squad spirit.

Dick Campbell began his coaching career at North Greenville Jr. College in Tigerville, South Carolina, where he won 135 games while losing only

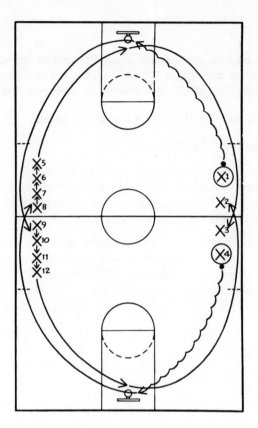

29. His teams were Western Carolina Junior College Champions from
1954 to 1958. When he left North Greenville he had won 50 consecutive
conference games. From there he went to Carson-Newman College in 1958.
His overall coaching record at Carson-Newman was 227 wins against 64
losses. His teams were Volunteer State Athletic Conference Champions in
1962, 1963, 1964, and 1965. They finished third in the NAIA Tournament in 1964. Coach Campbell was named the National Basketball Writers
Association NAIA Coach of the Year in 1965.

THREE-LINE LAYUP DRILL

Lenny Fant

Northeast Louisiana State College

**B1 passes to C1 and goes off his tail. C1 passes to A1 and rebounds. He
then throws the ball to B1 who has gone up the baseline. The feeder (A1)
goes to the C line. The rebounder (C1) goes to shooting line B. The**

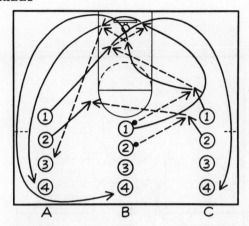

shooter goes to the A line. After B1 (shooter) gets the ball back from C1 (rebounder) he throws to A3. The ball then goes to B3 for the same procedure. As soon as B1 goes and shoots, B2 starts with B1 and B3 while the first ball is coming back to be used by A3-B3-C3. Two balls are used, and everyone must go back on the outside so as not to hit head on with the second group coming in.

Special Value of the Drill

1. Passing to cutter on move.
2. Receiving ball and shooting without a dribble.
3. Quick rotation without letting ball hit the floor.
4. A lot of players can be moved and worked at the same time.
5. You work on all types of layups.

Lenny Fant has set records for both success and longevity as basketball coach at Northeast since he arrived there in 1955. He has coached more years, won more games (140), won more conference championships (two), and enjoyed more winning seasons (seven) than any other Northeast coach. His program hit its stride in 1961–62 when he shocked the Gulf State Conference with a 17–8 season and the league title. His record at Northeast is 140–126, 105–64 over the past seven seasons.

FREE THROW SHOOTING STAR DRILL

Lee Fulmer

University of Redlands

This drill operates to maximum efficiency with 12 players and six baskets. Players work in pairs and will eventually shoot at three different baskets

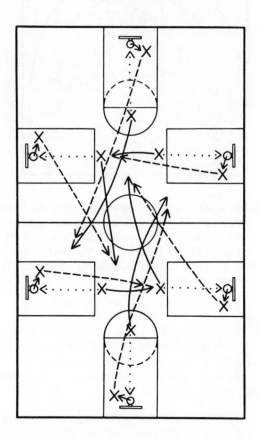

as they rotate. A player shoots two shots and takes off for his next basket as soon as he sees the players ahead starting to move from their basket. His partner throws him a long pass and he drives in for a layup or pulls up and feeds his partner who is trailing the pass for his layup shot. It is now the partner's turn to shoot his two free throws. After this he, in turn, takes off for the next basket, looking for the long pass from his partner and the driving layup or trailer opportunity. All six groups are doing this at the same time. Players will shoot a total of 26 free throws and appropriate incentives are used to reward accurate shooting. Complete records of the shooting are kept. This is an advanced type of free throw shooting drill and is not used daily, but probably once or twice a week at the most.

Special Value of the Drill

1. The players like it.
2. Free throws are shot after running—a game-like activity.
3. It teaches the player the importance of developing a routine before shooting.

4. It gives an opportunity for practice on other skills at the same time
   —long accurate passing, driving layups, and trailer opportunities
   for layup or short jumper.
5. Peripheral vision is a must.
6. It fits well into a 15-minute time slot for free throws.

*Lee Fulmer has been the basketball coach at the University of Redlands
since 1954. Under the guidance of Coach Fulmer, the Bulldogs have captured four SCIAC Championships and have shared the crown twice. Fulmer's teams compiled a 205–167 record against top competition and his
1961 Bulldog team was the first University of Redlands squad to win a
trip to the NAIA playoffs in Kansas City. The team made a return trip
three years later.*

SPOT SHOOTING DRILL

William Gibson
University of Virginia

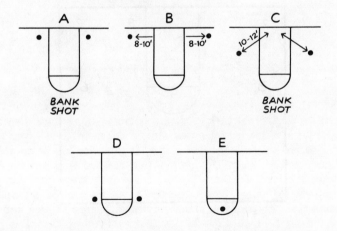

This drill is used daily. The total shooting time is five minutes (one minute at each letter). Three to four boys shoot at each basket. The players
start on a whistle and stop on the whistle. Each player has a basketball,
and each player rebounds his own shot. If the player starts on the right
side of the basket, after the shot he rebounds and shoots from the same
spot on the left side of the basket. The players try to get as many shots
as possible during the minute from the various spots.

Special Value of the Drill

These are in the areas where most shots are taken in the game, and through practice in recognizing the high percentage shot, the player will not hesitate to take it when the opportunity presents itself in a game. During the past season our three inside men shot 60%, 58%, and 57%!

After a successful high school career, William Gibson became the basketball coach at Mansfield State College in Pennsylvania. In seven seasons his teams recorded 102 wins against 37 losses, and two state championships. In his last three years at Mansfield, his teams won 58 games while losing only seven. In two successive years his teams led the nation in margin of difference (regarding point spread against the opponent). He then moved to the University of Virginia in 1963 as the head coach.

BASKETBALL GOLF GAME

Larry Hanson

Jefferson High School, Los Angeles, California

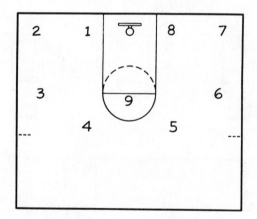

Two players pair off. Player 1 receives a pass from player 2 in the 1 spot. Player 2 then counts as fast as he can (1–2–3). If he can complete the three-count before player 1 gets the shot off, one *stroke* or shot is charged. Player 1 keeps shooting until he makes it at station 1. Player 2 is keeping score. Then player 2 at station 1 does the same and on through to station 9. Station 9 is a free throw spot and the players shoot

until they make it. The stations are arranged to correspond to weak spots in various zones. The three-count helps players practice quick shooting.

Special Value of the Drill

The contest between players causes experience under pressure. Before the season ends many perfect scores of nine have been recorded. A bulletin board of "Best Golfers of Nine" for the season is kept for the players who have made it. The scoring and the recording of the scores for the game of the day cause concentration to become an important factor since all squad members are competing at the same time. The game can be played by players on their own time. Players are always shooting for the perfect score of nine. Shooting really improves!

Larry Hanson's amazing coaching career began at El Centro High School where, during three years of basketball, his teams won 97 games and lost only three, winning six Imperial Valley Championships. He moved to Reedley Junior College and in two years won 50 games and lost only two. His teams captured two C.C.J.C. League Championships. He then came to Jefferson High School in Los Angeles, California, where in 24 years (coaching two teams each year) his winning percentage is 92%. This record includes 40 championships, eight of which are Los Angeles City Championships. In two consecutive years (1965 and 1966), his teams averaged over 100 points per game—105.2 in 1965 and 115.1 in 1966.

PRE-GAME DRILL

Barry Holtgrewe

Storm Lake High School, Storm Lake, Iowa

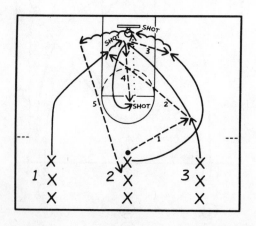

A man from line 2 passes to the man at the head of line 3 who is cutting
to the basket. The line 3 man in turn passes to a man from line 1 cutting
in for the shot. The number 2 man hesitates for a moment and then cuts
for the basket, receiving a pass from number 3 who has rebounded number 1's layup. Number 3 continues out to 15 or 18 feet anywhere around
the perimeter and takes a pass from number 1. Number 3 then takes a
jump shot. Number 2 rebounds this shot and passes out. The players
move to the right.

Special Value of the Drill

This is a good pre-game drill because it combines running, passing, and
shooting. It is used as the third pre-game drill after the players have shot
partner layups and run through the one-line continuous tipping maneuver.

Barry Holtgrewe began his coaching career at Granby High School in Nor-
folk, Virginia, in 1959. In two seasons he compiled a record of 33 wins
and 12 losses and finished second in the state tournament. In 1961 he
moved to Storm Lake High School in Storm Lake, Iowa, where he has re-
corded 138 wins against 45 losses. During this time he has won five con-
ference championships and his teams have appeared in the state tourna-
ment on four occasions, finishing fifth twice, fourth once, and winning the
state crown once.

THREE-LINE PRE-GAME WARM-UP DRILL

Rex Hughes

Assistant Coach, University of Nebraska

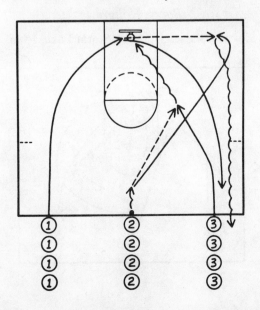

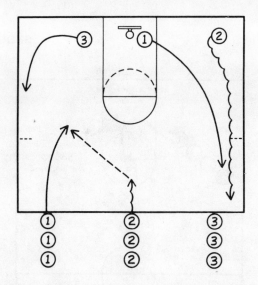

(2) dribbles past half court and passes to (3) who shoots the layup. (2) then continues to the corner. (1) rebounds the ball and passes to (2) in the corner. (2) pivots to the outside and dribbles quickly up the court. After rebounding and passing out, (1) chases (2) to bother his dribbling up court. (1) rotates to line 2, (2) rotates to line 3, and (3) rotates to line one. As soon as the pass is made to the corner, the next (3) player may go. Alternate to the right, then to the left.

Special Value of the Drill

1. Right- and left-hand *full speed* layup.
2. Outlet passes to corner and foul line extended.
3. Dribbling with pressure both right- and left-handed.
4. Ball handling.
5. Used as a pre-game warm-up.

After four seasons at Redondo High School, where he won 82 games while losing 30 and was three times voted "Coach of the Year" in the Bay League, Rex Hughes moved to Long Beach City College. In his first year he compiled a record of 23 wins against only five losses. In 1969 he became the assistant coach at the University of Nebraska in Lincoln, Nebraska.

TEN-POINT DRILL

Jack Jackson

Gulf Coast Junior College

The squad is divided into three equal groups. Each group will have a ball with three balls at the opposite end of the floor on the free throw line.

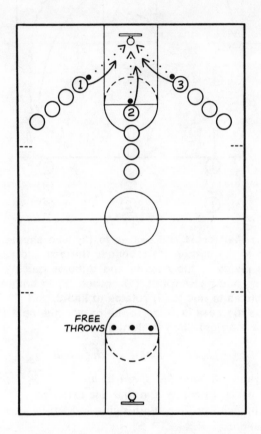

The game is played to 20 baskets. On the signal from the coach, the front three players will shoot jump shots, attempting to make the shot. If they miss, they try to rebound the missed shot in the air. If successful they are permitted a second shot. If the first shot is missed and the player fails to rebound the ball in the air, he must sprint down and make a free throw before he returns. If both shots are missed, the player will sprint to the opposite end and must make a free throw before returning to his line. Emphasize at all times that the players make good passes back to their line after a shot.

Special Value of the Drill

1. To improve spot shooting.
2. To improve receiving the ball with good set position.
3. Shooting quickly with eyes on the rim.
4. Develop relaxation and confidence in the offensive player when under pressure.

5. To develop the different passes.
6. To learn to follow the shot.
7. Second effort rebounding.
8. To improve free throw shooting.
9. Good conditioning drill.
10. A very effective competitive drill.

After one year as freshman coach at Eastern Kentucky University, Jack Jackson became the basketball coach at Gulf Coast Junior College in Panama City, Florida. In his first season at Gulf Coast, Coach Jackson's team tied the school record for most wins in a season (21). He then broke the record in his second and third years with records of 23–7 and 24–7. His overall coaching record now stands at 102 wins and 29 losses.

CIRCUIT SHOOTING DRILL

John Kicklighter

St. Andrew's High School, Charleston, South Carolina

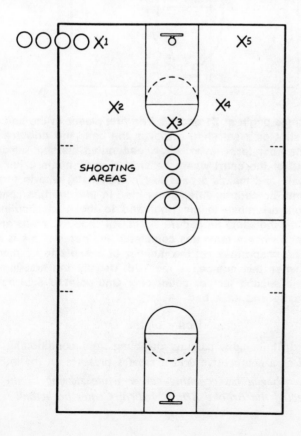

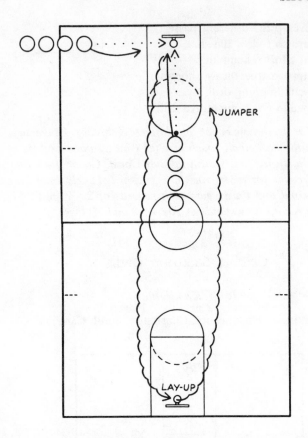

Two shooting lines begin at X1 and X3. The first player in the line shoots
either a jump shot or a set shot, retrieves the ball, and dribbles to the
other end of the floor for a layup. After rebounding his shot he dribbles
back to the end of the court where he started and shoots a jump shot,
retrieves the ball, and makes a pass to his teammate, who in turn goes
through the same procedure. After every man in the line has completed
the drill, the players move to the right and to the next shooting spot
where they follow the same procedure again. All shooting areas are used
and the drill ends when a team has completed the circuit. This is a competitive drill. The coach may set the number of baskets to be made and
the drill ends when this number is reached. Usually the first jumper or
set shot and the second jumper count one. One point is subtracted for
each missed layup and each bad pass.

Special Value of the Drill

This shooting drill includes passing, dribbling, and conditioning values.
When installed as a competitive drill it creates pressure on the individual.
*John Kicklighter began his coaching career while serving in the armed
forces. He directed the Brooke Army Medical Center basketball team for*

three seasons. After this he became head basketball coach at St. Andrew's Parish High School in Charleston, South Carolina. In seven years at St. Andrew's, Coach Kicklighter's record is 111–36 and includes two state titles and two state runner-up spots. He was named "Coach of the Year" in 1965 and 1968. In 1966 he directed the South All-Star Basketball team.

LONG PASS DRILL

John MacLeod

University of Oklahoma

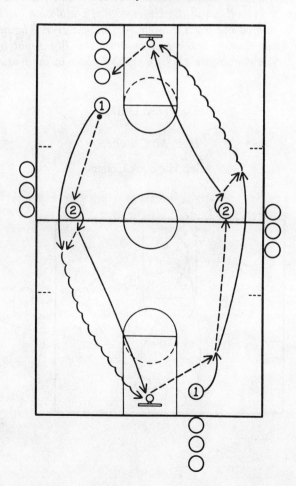

The drill begins with #1 passing to #2, who has stepped to the ten-second line to receive the pass. #1 throws the pass and #2 then hands the ball back to #1 as he drives in for a one-hand layup. #2 then becomes the rebounder and passes to the next #1 man as the drill continues. #2 then goes to the 1 line and #1, who shot the ball, now goes to the 2 line. The drill may be used to shoot from the left-hand side also.

Special Value of the Drill

We use this drill as a substitute for sprints at the conclusion of practice. We feel that there is value in letting the boys open up and go as hard as they can possibly go. At the same time they get an opportunity to shoot the layup at full speed. The kids get a big kick out of this drill with a lot of hand-clapping and shouting going on as they try to encourage each player to go faster and try a little harder.

After a successful high school coaching career, John MacLeod accepted the freshman basketball job at the University of Oklahoma in 1966. In his first season he guided the frosh to their best season ever. The next year he became the head Sooner coach and stunned the Big Eight by finishing 13–13 and 8–6 in conference play for a third place in the league.

CENTER DRILL

Bob McCutchen

Allan Hancock College

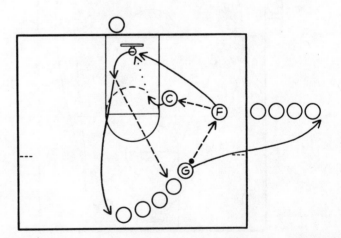

The guard passes to the forward and the forward in turn passes quickly to the center posted inside for a shot. The forward rebounds and throws out to the next person in the guard line. Two balls are used. The players keep the center hustling with quick passes almost before he has time to recover after his shot. The center shoots approximately ten shots before he is replaced by another player standing behind the baseline. The outside players go to the opposite side of the floor and change positions each time so that they can learn to operate from both the guard and forward position on each side of the court.

Special Value of the Drill

This is a good drill to develop a center's moves around the basket. It is important that a team have a strong inside game and a center who has a variety of moves with real accuracy and polish. No one man should be able to stop him. The drill also gives the outside man practice in hitting the center accurately and with good, crisp passes.

In nine seasons at Santa Maria High School in California, Bob McCutchen's winning percentage was better than 85%. During this time his teams won eight conference championships and two California Interscholastic Federation titles. In the 1966–67 season he moved to Allan Hancock College in Santa Maria. During three seasons there his winning percentage is 74% and includes two conference championships.

COMPETITIVE SHOOTING DRILL

Jack McKinney

St. Joseph's College

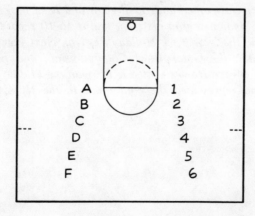

This is a shooting drill with some rules to make it interesting. Two teams are shooting against each other in a long and short game of 30. Two points are given for a long shot, one point for a layup. Three points are subtracted for a missed layup. The players do not get the layup until after they have made the first jump shot (long). After making their first jumper they are then allowed a layup every time, even if they miss the next jump shot. Ball interference (one ball hitting another ball around the hoop) does not count for –3 points if the layup is missed, but the shooter gets no second layup. There are three games. The winner is the team who wins two out of three games. The losers must run laps. The number of laps is determined by two competing teams before the start of the game. Every score must be announced verbally with running score by one member of each team (team scorekeeper).

Special Value of the Drill

It is a great shooting drill because it emphasizes pressure shooting, following the shot, and is very spirited and competitive. We do this the day before every game, with the two teams being picked by the co-captains before the season starts. The teams remain the same the whole year. A cumulative score is kept and after the last game the losers for the year must buy the winners a dinner. It fosters great team spirit.

Starting with his playing career at St. Joseph's under Dr. Jack Ramsey, and through the past three seasons as head coach, Jack McKinney's teams have won over 70% of their games. He played for Coach Ramsey on the Hawk varsity from 1954 through 1957. In 1960 he returned to St. Joseph's as freshman basketball coach. In five years as frosh mentor he rang up a record of 59–18 and two Big Five titles. In 1965 he took his first major coaching job at Philadelphia Textile. In his only season there he led the Rams to a 20–6 slate and a berth in the NCAA College Division Tournament. In 1966 he was named athletic director and head basketball coach at St. Joseph's. In his first season his team had a 16-10 record and won the runner-up spot in the New York Holiday Festival. Next year his team won the Big Five title, the Gator Bowl Championship, and posted a 17–9 record. In 1968–69 the Hawks went 17–11, won the Middle Atlantic Conference title, and represented the conference in the NCAA tournament.

PRE-GAME SPECIAL WARM-UP DRILL

Charles Obye
Morningside College

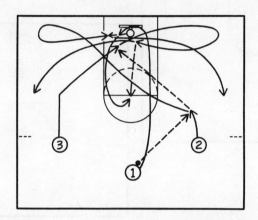

(1) makes a chest pass to (2) and follows his pass. (2) bounce passes to (3) for a driving layup and follows his pass to the opposite corner. (1) rebounds (3)'s layup and flip passes to (2) for a baseline layup, and then continues to the free throw line. (3) rebounds (2)'s layup and throws an outlet pass to (1) for a jump shot. (1) rebounds his own shot and outlets with a baseball pass to either (2) or (3).

Special Value of the Drill

The drill provides the layup and jump shooting practice coming from the quick break. A variety of passes are used. Offensive play continues from the rebound. It is a good warm-up drill for pre-game sessions.

Charles Obye began his coaching career as an assistant coach at Morningside College in Sioux City, Iowa. In 1949 he began an eight-year tenure as head coach at Wayne State College in Nebraska. In 1957 his team won the Nebraska College Conference Championship and the NAIA District Championship. The next season he returned to Morningside College as the head coach. Included in his 12-year record at Morningside is a District #15 NAIA Championship in 1959.

Partner Shooting Drill

Dr. Richard Sauers
Albany State University

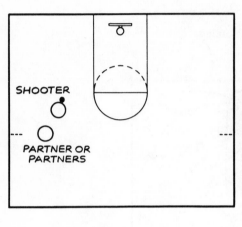

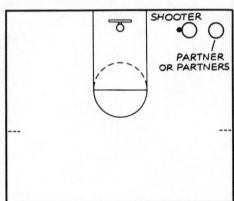

The drill requires a basketball and a basket for each two or three players. Each group of two or three is a team competing against the others for a prescribed length of time (one and a half to two minutes seems to be best). Each group shoots at a different basket after each game, completing the circuit of five or six baskets. The angle of the shot varies at each basket (baseline, 45 degree, head on, etc). The shooter follows his shot. A made shot counts three points—a tip-in with one or two hands also counts three points if it is on the first effort—a second effort tip-in counts two points—another follow-up counts one point. The ball is passed quickly back to the next shooter. Score is kept and a winning team is declared.

Special Value of the Drill

The drill gets players to shoot quickly after receiving a pass. It is competitive and very popular with the players. The drill makes players shoot from different angles (including the use of the backboard).

Dr. Richard Sauers has been at Albany State University since 1955. Under his leadership, Albany has posted a record of 224–104. This includes five Capital City Championships, one NAIA Christmas Championship, and one appearance in the NCAA Eastern Regionals.

"21" GAME

Bill Sharman

Los Angeles Stars

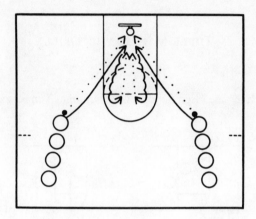

Two teams of players line up approximately 20 to 25 feet from the basket. Each player receives two shots per turn and gets credit for one point for each basket scored. The team that scores 21 points first wins the game. Each player takes a long shot, retrieves his own shot, and then dribbles to the free throw line for a second shot. He again follows his shot, rebounds, and passes back to his teammate.

Special Value of the Drill

This is an excellent competitive shooting drill. It encourages accuracy along with speed in shooting.

The greatest free throw shooter in the history of the National Basketball Association was Bill Sharman, whose 93.2% on 342 out of 367 attempts during the 1958–59 season with the Boston Celtics still remains the all-time high. He also holds the NBA record for consecutive free throws, hitting 56 straight in 1959 during the playoffs and 55 straight during the 1957 season. His 88.3% is the NBA top mark for a career. During his ten-year period he averaged 17.8 points per game. He coached the San Francisco Warriors for two seasons. His team defeated the St. Louis Hawks in the first round of the 1968 NBA playoffs before losing to the Lakers in the division final. In 1966–67 the Warriors whipped the Lakers and Hawks to win the Western Division title but lost to the 76'ers in the finals. In 1961–62 he served as head coach of the Los Angeles Jets for a half season and for the Cleveland Pipers for a half season. From 1962–64 he was the head coach at Cal State Los Angeles. His popular book Sharman on Basketball Shooting *was recently issued in paperback by Prentice-Hall.*

Three-Man Layup Drill

Dorsey Sims

Riverside High School, Chattanooga, Tennessee

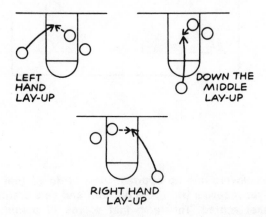

Most modern gymnasiums have extra side baskets, and by putting three players at each basket, more individual work can be accomplished. Usually a squad of 15 to 20 players can work at the same time. The coach will be able to find out very quickly who can, and who cannot, use both hands, who can use the boards, and who can lay it over the front rim lip with the soft touch.

Special Value of the Drill

This drill develops left-hand driving layup accuracy, right-hand layup accuracy, rebounding, passing to driving cutter, quickness in getting into position to cut for the basket and receive a pass, and also serves as an excellent conditioner.

Dorsey Sims Jr. took the reins at Riverside High School in Chattanooga, Tennessee, just four days before the start of regular season practice. Since that time Coach Sims' Trojans have won two back-to-back TSSAA State

Tournaments (1968 and 1969), a fourth place in 1967, and established an all-time TSSAA record of 60 straight wins. His teams have stacked up trophies and records of 18–10, 27–3, 32–2, and 33–0. Counting a 27–20 record at McReynolds High School, a 99–26 mark at Slater High School, and his 110–15 ledger at Riverside, Coach Sims has an 11-year record of 236–61. He was selected Coach of the Year in the Hamilton Interscholastic League in 1967, 1968, and 1969. He was the coach of the East Tennessee All-Stars in 1969.

WEAK-SIDE SHOOTING DRILL

Dr. Robert White

Wisconsin State University

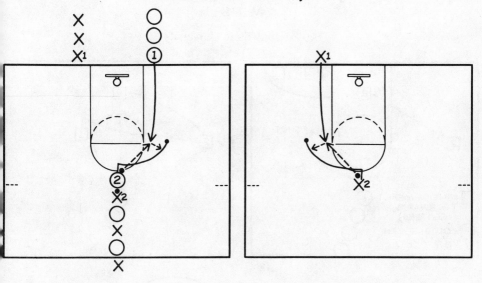

O1 comes high along the baseline and receives a pass from O2. O2 takes a jab step to the foul line and comes over O1 for the pass back and the jump shot. O1 rolls to the basket for a return pass or the rebound. Using a second ball, X2 passes to X1 at the side post and cuts over the top for the same shot or pass on the pick and roll. Players rotate positions.

Special Value of the Drill

This drill helps players become conscious of the weak-side game. It involves good passing and footwork as well as good shooting practice. On occasion, the hand-off man puts some pressure on the shooter. We also

like the drill because it involves several people and brings about movement
on the part of the shooter.

*Robert White began his coaching career as an assistant coach at Brush
High School in Cleveland, Ohio. He then moved to University High
School at Ohio State University where he remained for seven years, com-
piling a record of 101 wins against 31 losses. While at University High
School he won three county, three sectional, and two district champion-
ships. In 1964 he became the head basketball coach at Wisconsin State
University in Oshkosh. During five seasons at Wisconsin State, he recorded
74 wins against 44 losses and two conference and two District 14 Cham-
pionships. His team was third in the National NAIA Tourney and Dr.
White received "Coach of the Year" honors in 1967 and 1968.*

DUAL JUMP SHOT DRILL

Ned Wulk

Arizona State University

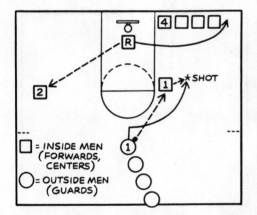
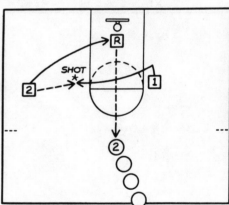
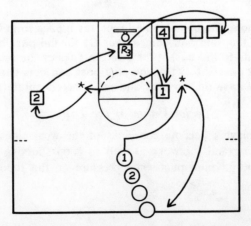

[ ] = inside men (forwards and centers)   ( ) = outside men (guards)

Outside jump shot (Diagram #1) (1) feeds to [1] at side post, uses a cut-off move, gets the ball back from [1] and takes a jump shot off the screen. [R] rebounds that shot, passes to [2] to initiate jump shot for inside. [R] goes to the end of [4] line.

Inside jump shot (Diagram #2 [2] receives ball from [R] after outside jump shot. He feeds to [1] cutting across the lane for come-across jump shot. [2] now rebounds that shot, returns the ball to (2) in outside shooting line and stays as [R] for next outside jump shot. The drill now starts the second round. *Rotation for dual jump shot drill* (Diagram #3) *Inside men*: Go from end of [ ] line to [1], receive pass from (1), hand back to him for jump shot. After [2] has ball, cut across lane and get pass from [2] for jump shot. Go to [2] spot, receive pass from [R] and feed to next inside man coming across lane, rebounding that shot at [R] and then throwing the ball out to (2) line. Then stay there for outside jump shot and rebound. *Outside men*: (1) feeds [1], cuts off, gets ball back and takes jump shot at side of the key. After the shot, return to end of ( ) line.

Special Value of the Drill

This drill utilizes *two* types of jump shots adapted to inside men and to the outside men. They are precise shots used in a set offensive pattern. The advantage is in the two types of shots used.

Ned Wulk came to Arizona State University in 1957. His record since that time is 177 wins against 119 losses. In his first year, the Devils won the Border Conference crown. In the four seasons that followed, ASU was champion, co-champion, tri-champion, and runner-up. The 1960–61 squad drove to the finals of the NCAA Western Regionals. Wulk's 1962–63 team achieved a rating of third best in the nation and posted a 26–3 record. They recorded the first league title in the WAC and again were finalists in the NCAA Western Regionals. During the 1963–64 season the Sun Devils were conference co-champs.

REACTION—DRIVE LAYUP DRILL

Rudy Yaksich

Toronto High School, Toronto, Ohio

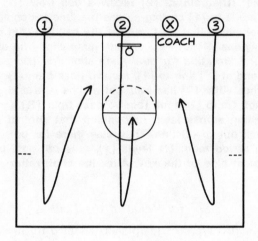

Three players line up along the baseline. On the coach's signal they sprint toward midcourt. The coach calls the name of one of the players. On the call the players change directions and come back toward the baseline. The player whose name was called looks for the ball and the other two become the defense and try to stop the man in his drive to the basket. The coach stands at the baseline and tosses the ball anywhere in the back court after making the call to change the players' direction.

Special Value of the Drill

The drill teaches quick reaction in getting a loose ball and quick adjustment by players to defense. Aggressive play can be developed.

Rudy Yaksich began his coaching career at Adena (Ohio) High School where he recorded 58 wins against 43 losses and the Eastern Ohio Athletic League title. He moved to Brilliant Memorial High School in 1965, and his free-lance system of play brought the league championship in 1966. In 1968 he became the basketball coach at Toronto High School in Toronto, Ohio. Coach Yaksich is the author of the book Winning Basketball with the Free-Lance System *(Parker Publishing Company).*

Two-Man Close-out Shooting Drill

Homer Zugelder

Hillsdale High School, San Mateo, California

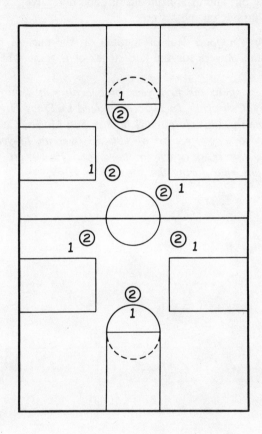

1 passes the ball to (2) from the end line. 1 closes out to guard (2). 1 assumes a good defensive stance with the hand upraised and the body balanced. (2) now shoots the ball as in a game-like situation. After (2) has shot the ball, 1 will make contact and block out momentarily (to create the habit of blocking out). (2) will rebound his own shot. As (2) is rebounding his own shot, 1 may move anywhere he wishes on the floor. (2) now rebounds and quickly finds 1, making a good outlet pass to him. Now (2) closes out to a good defensive position with the hand raised and the body balanced. 1 now shoots over (2) and the drill continues. Four players can work on one basket if space is a factor.

Special Value of the Drill

This drill incorporates many important aspects of good basketball:

1. Game-like shooting.
2. Outlet passing.
3. Closing out and establishment of good defensive position.
4. Blocking out on the shooter.

The drill requires a good deal of stamina on the part of the players. It helps prepare the players for the late stages of a game when fatigue is a factor.

Homer Zugelder spent his first year of coaching at Tracy Junior High School in Tracy, California. In 1956 he moved to Tracy High School, and in 1957 he came to Hillsdale High School in San Mateo, California, where he has recorded a league record of 106–38 over an 11-year period. He was selected as the West coach in the annual East-West All-Star game in Northern California during the summer of 1969.

2

Passing Drills

A great many coaches claim that passing in basketball is a lost art. As a highly complex skill, it requires much time and attention to detail. There are several key ingredients necessary for success: good timing, anticipation, knowledge of the game, quickness, peripheral vision, and accuracy. Good passing also requires good receiving. Coordinating the efforts of two or more men in this area of play is essential.

FULL SPEED PASSING AND SHOOTING DRILL

Edward Ashnault

Colgate University

Six players (X) line up as shown. The remainder of the squad lines up on the end line and the drill proceeds with four or five balls. The first man on end line passes to X1, then receives a pass back and passes to X2 who in turn passes it back. The ball is then passed to X3 and back for a layup. The shooter takes his own rebound and passes to X4, X5, and X6, each time receiving a return pass. He finishes with a layup. As many repetitions as the coach desires may be run before changing personnel. The drill should be used from both sides of end line for left and right layups.

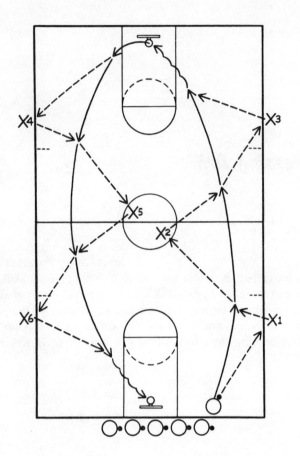

Special Value of the Drill

The drill is great for conditioning and for receiving and passing at full speed. It also provides practice in shooting layups after a pass taken at full speed involving both the right and left hand. Without quick hands the man running will outrun the passes.

Edward Ashnault was named head coach of basketball at Colgate University in 1967 after a three-year tenure in the same position at Dickinson College in Carlisle, Pennsylvania. His record at Dickinson was 40–21, and included the southern division title of the Middle Atlantic Conference in 1964–65. He began his coaching career at Wilton (Connecticut) High School, where his basketball teams captured the Western Connecticut Championship in three of his four years with a remarkable record of 77 wins, nine losses, including a streak of 38 victories.

Four-corner Pass and Shoot Drill

Robert Basarich

Lockport Central High School, Lockport, Illinois

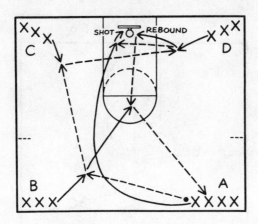

**The players line up in the four corners of a half court. The longest line
should be the shooting line. Line A starts with the ball and passes to B
(two-hand chest pass). B breaks out from the corner to receive the pass.
B pivots on the left foot and passes to C, using a two-hand over-the-head
pass. C breaks out from the corner to receive the ball. C pivots on the
left foot and passes to D, using a bounce pass. D breaks out from the
corner to receive the pass. After A passes to B, he begins running behind B and then breaks for the basket and shoots a left-handed layup.
After D receives the ball from C he passes to A with either a flip pass or
a bounce pass. D rebounds the shot and then passes to B at the free
throw line. B pivots and returns the ball to the shooting line. Players
rotate by going to the line to whom they first passed. A goes to B, B to C,
etc. After each player has shot once, the direction is reversed so that
the players can shoot a right-handed layup. The drill can be run with one
or two balls.**

Special Value of the Drill

The drill teaches at least three different passes; it teaches timing and a
player coming to meet the ball; and it teaches pivoting, catching, and
shooting the ball on the move.

*In three years of coaching basketball, Robert Basarich compiled an amaz-
ing 77 wins against only nine defeats. At Lockport Central High School
in Lockport, Illinois, he had seasons of 24–5, 28–2, and 25–2. His teams
have won three straight conference titles, three regional titles, and played
in three sectional finals, winning one.*

Pass Through Drill

Jim Cathcart

Little Rock Central High School, Little Rock, Arkansas

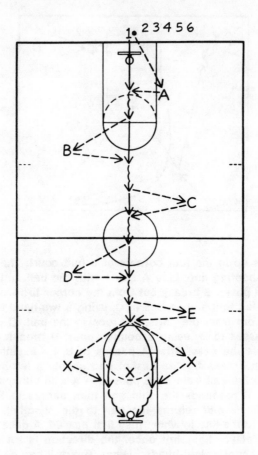

Players A through E are stationed on the court in the positions illustrated. The player starting at the end line passes to each of these players and receives a return pass as he moves down the court toward the basket at the other end. The coach is represented by the X and can place himself in the middle of the free throw circle about three feet below the free throw line, or he can move to either side of the lane extended about four to five feet. This allows the players to get the layup on the right or the layup on the left. If the coach wants his players to have a little more time to receive the pass and in return make a good pass, he can space players A through E at a wider distance. This will help them make the adjustment with their feet as well as making a good

fundamental pass. If the coach wants the passing to pick up, he can move the players in closer. This forces them to execute the pass much more quickly as well as adjusting their feet to shorter steps. As soon as group 1 finishes, they can turn and go the other way toward the basket at the other end of the court. Then they can take the places of the passers A through E while those players go through the drill.

Special Value of the Drill

It is an excellent drill for giving players experience in passing and receiving while moving quickly down the court. It moves very quickly, and a large number of players can take part.

Jim Cathcart began his coaching career at the University of Arkansas where he was the freshman basketball coach for one season. He then moved to Southwest Jr. High School in Little Rock, Arkansas, where he won the city championship. After this he became head basketball coach at Little Rock Central High School. In five seasons there he compiled a record of 85 wins against 26 losses. Included in this record are two invitational championships, a AAA Conference Championship, and a AAA State Championship. He is the author of A Multiple-Continuous Offense for High School Basketball *(Parker Publishing Company).*

FOUR-CORNER PASSING DRILL

Dan Fukushima

James Lick High School, San Jose, California

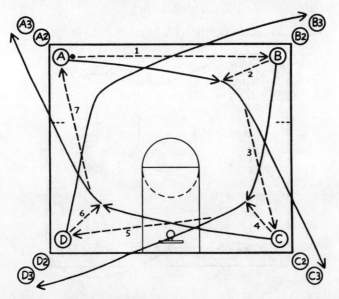

**A passes to B and runs toward him and gets a return pass, then passes
to C and retires to the end of C line. In the meantime, B cuts off A's tail,
takes a pass from C and passes to D and retires to the end of D line.
C cuts off B's tail, receives a pass from D and passes to A2 and retires
to the end of A line. A2 cuts off D's tail, receives a return pass from B2
and passes to C2 and so on. It looks complicated but it is extremely
simple. Players learn in a few minutes. You can call the rotation in reverse, or even put another ball into the drill.**

Special Value of the Drill

This is an extremely colorful drill that stresses speed, accuracy, timing,
reaction, and conditioning—everything that is desirable in a passing drill.
The values derived are directly applicable to game situations. Players enjoy
it and take pride in executing it, and insist on using it as a part of pre-game
warmup. The drill is very easy to teach, and can be used best with anywhere from eight to 18 players.

*A veteran of more than 20 years as a basketball coach is Dan Fukushima,
whose varsity teams at James Lick High School have had only one losing
season during his tenure there. In 1964 he was invited to stage a series of
clinics throughout the empire by the Japan Amateur Basketball Association. He was invited for a repeat series in 1967 and 1971. During the summer of 1968 he was designated coach of the West All-Stars in the Northern California East-West All-Star Game.*

FOUR-CORNER FLIP PASS DRILL

Bruce Gehrke

Mineola High School, Mineola, New York

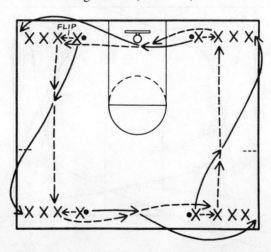

Players are divided into four equal groups spaced ten yards apart. At least three men must be in each group. A ball is given to the first man in each group. The coach designates the direction in which the players will move. At a starting signal, the first man turns and flips a short two-handed pass (underhand) to the second man in his group. The first man immediately runs to the next group looking for a return pass (two-handed chest pass or whatever type pass the players need work on), from the second man in his group to whom he had just flipped the ball. This pass must come as quickly as possible. As the first man catches the ball, he passes to the man in the next group (originally the second man) and becomes the last man in that group. This is continued as long as the coach desires. On a signal the direction may be reversed. At first it might be advisable to start with one ball and progress to four as the group demonstrates ability to handle the drill. The drill must be begun anew after a fumble or a bad pass.

Special Value of the Drill

The drill emphasizes quick, accurate passes and reaction. It puts a premium on getting the ball quickly and accurately into the man's hands, enabling him to make the next pass as quickly as possible. It keeps the entire group on their toes because there are only seconds between passing and catching.

Bruce Gehrke's outstanding record includes 20 years of coaching experience at Mineola High School in Long Island, New York, where he has recorded 281 wins against 105 losses, and eight league championships.

FOUR-CORNER PASS AND GO DRILL

George Ireland
Loyola of Chicago

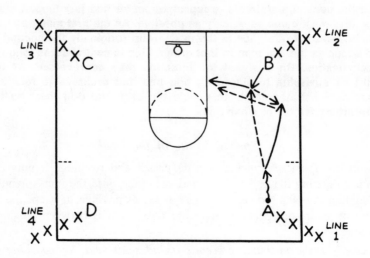

**A passes to B, A moves toward B, B returns pass to A, B moves toward
C, A returns pass to B, B passes to C, C returns pass to B, B passes to C.
This process keeps going so that all four corners are covered. The
players start with one ball, but another is added until four balls are in
motion at the same time. While drill is in motion, blow whistle to reverse.**

Special Value of the Drill

The drill simulates game conditions. The men are moving under pressure
and if all passes are not perfect and going at top speed, someone will be
hit in the head. The players like it. It develops all types of passes and excellent footwork.

*George Ireland, the winningest coach in the history of Loyola basketball,
has led his teams to 268 wins gainst 175 losses in 18 seasons for a .605
winning percentage. Coach Ireland, a member of the Helms Athletic Foundation Hall of Fame, began his coaching career in Aurora, Illinois, a
suburb of Chicago. He compiled a record of 270 wins against 78 losses
at Marmion Military Academy. His 1963 Loyola team won the NCAA
Championship.*

Two-on-One Passing Drill

Ray Krzoska

University of Wisconsin, Milwaukee

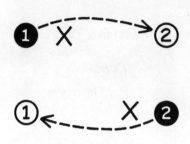

O1 and O2 are approximately 15 feet apart and facing each other. X1 is in a normal defensive stance. The team is divided into groups of three which are spread around the floor.

No dribble is allowed. (Later the coach may allow one or two dribbles as part of a fake.) O1 and O2 are allowed only one step. O1 uses many different fakes with eyes, head, shoulders, movable foot, and ball trying to pass over, under, or through the defensive man. O2 waits until defensive man is ready and then tries to get the pass back to O1. (This is not a chase for the middle man.) The players change positions after an interception or after a certain amount of time has elapsed or a number of passes have been made.

Special Value of the Drill

1. This is an excellent passing drill.
2. It encourages the use of many different types of passes.
3. It encourages development and use of fakes to get the defensive man out of position.
4. This is a good one-on-one defensive drill for the man in the middle.

The captain of the only undefeated basketball team in the modern history of the University of Wisconsin at Milwaukee, Ray Krzoska guided the Panthers for six seasons as their basketball coach. He joined the UWM staff in 1957 as intramural director and became head basketball coach in 1963. He won all-league acclaim each of his four seasons as a cager at Milwaukee State, and captained the 1940–41 team.

Baseline Drill

Don Odle
Taylor University

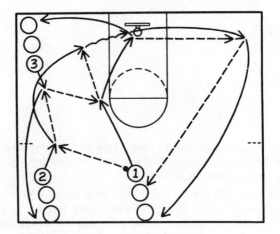

Player 1 passes to 2 who in turn passes to 3 moving out from the corner. 3 flips the ball to number 1 at the corner of the lane near the free throw line extended. Number 2, after passing to 3, breaks around him and cuts toward the basket. After receiving a pass from number 1, he shoots the layup. Player 1 rebounds the ball and passes to number 2 moving into the corner after his shot. On the rotation, number 1 moves to the 3 line, number 2 moves to the 1 line, and number 3 moves to the 2 line.

Special Value of the Drill

This is an excellent drill to develop good passing habits and to help players learn to coordinate their movements. It utilizes a large number of players and gives them work in several areas of basketball play.

Don Odle has guided Taylor University basketball for 20 seasons. During this time he had led his teams to three Hoosier Conference Championships and has won 21 different tournaments. For 12 years he took a group of college stars on basketball tours to the Orient and South America. This unprecedented program, known as Venture for Victory, was awarded a medal by the Freedom Foundation of America, was acclaimed by Look *magazine, and was cited in Congress. The VV teams have compiled a record of 650 wins against 28 losses. Held in high esteem in the Orient, Odle coached the Chinese Nationalist basketball team in the 1960 Olympics at the request of the Chinese government.*

FULL COURT PIVOT AND PASS DRILL

Dave Smalley

U.S. Naval Academy

X1 starts drill with a two-hand chest pass to (1), breaks down the middle and gets a return pass from (1). X1 immediately stops, reverse pivots, and passes to (2), after which he breaks down the floor again. (2) returns the pass to X1 who stops and reverse pivots again. X1 then hits (3), gets a return pass from (3), and shoots a layup. X2 steps on floor and passes to his right to (4). The same sequence then follows. The same drill can be worked to the left for left-handed layups. The coach should insist that the players run it at full speed and allow no dribbling.

Special Value of the Drill

The drill teaches pivoting, good body balance, and passing—three fundamentals often overlooked.

Ex-Navy great Dave Smalley has completed three seasons as head basketball coach of the Midshipmen. Smalley was assistant to Ben Carnevale for four seasons before taking the helm in March of 1966 when Carnevale

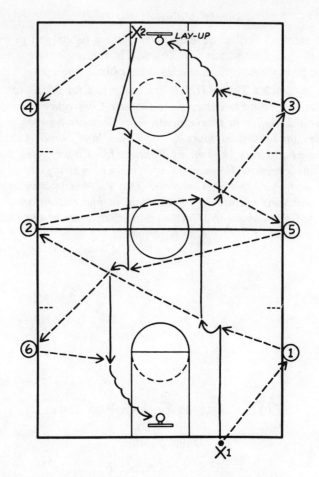

left to become Director of Athletics at New York University. A three-time letterman, Dave Smalley is one of only two cagers in Navy history to be elected captain two consecutive seasons. He was the Midshipmen's top scorer two of his three years on the varsity.

DIAMOND PASSING DRILL

Joe Sterling

Seminole Junior College

The team is divided into four lines (a diamond alignment). The player with the ball who begins the action may pass to any line and follow the

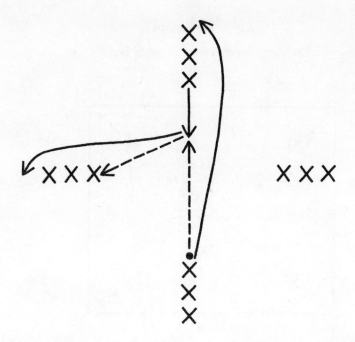

pass. **The receiver must move to the ball when he sees the pass coming to him. After receiving the pass, that player follows the same procedure.**

Special Value of the Drill

This drill teaches the players to move to meet the pass; failure to do so is one of the biggest faults of most players. Players standing and waiting for the pass causes a great deal of trouble offensively; this fault must be overcome. The drill described here is used daily. A great emphasis is placed on the importance of this obligation.

Joe Sterling began his coaching career in Greensboro High School in Greensboro, Florida, where he recorded 25 wins against three losses. His team won the 1951 Class "C" State Championship. In 1951 he moved to Apopka High School and in 15 seasons compiled 294 wins against 103 losses. In 1962 his team won the Class "A" State Championship. In 1966 he became the head basketball coach at Seminole Junior College in Sanford, Florida. In three seasons at Seminole his teams recorded 70 wins against only 11 losses, and were the Florida Junior College champions in 1969. This gives Coach Sterling the rare distinction of having had a state championship basketball team in each of the schools in which he has worked as head coach.

FOUR-CORNER PASSING DRILL

Jerry Tarkanian

California State College at Long Beach

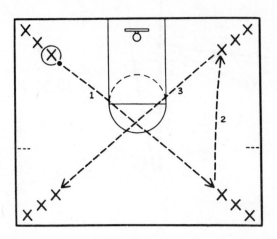

1. **First pass is directly across.**
2. **Second pass is to the right.**
3. **Players follow their pass, going to the end of the line to which they pass.**

Special Value of the Drill

1. The drill develops good passing habits.
2. Players learn to catch and pass on the move.
3. Any type of pass can be used. Players learn to perfect all types. Hand-offs may also be used when the lines are moved closer together.

Jerry Tarkanian joined the Cal State Long Beach staff in March of 1968. In his first season with the 49'ers he produced the school's first conference champion as the team finished the season with a 23–3 record. Prior to joining the Cal State Long Beach staff he compiled the finest junior college coaching record in the nation. During his years at Riverside and Pasadena City Colleges his teams won four straight California State Championships and were runners-up in a bid for a fifth. He started his coaching career with five years of high school at San Joaquin Memorial, Antelope Valley, and Redlands High Schools. He then went to Riverside City College and won the state title three years (1963 through 1966). In 1966–67 he moved to Pasadena City College and took a team that won three games the previous year. His first year he won the state title and followed that with a second place in overtime the next year. His record from the 1962 season through the 1969 season is a phenomenal 221–16!

BALL HANDLING DRILL

Frank Truitt

Kent State University

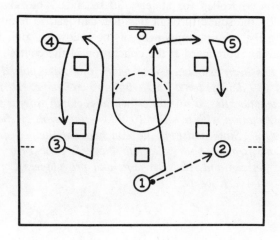

This drill takes ten men and a stop watch. There are no shots allowed and only two dribbles. The object is to control the ball as long as possible. All five players are constantly on the move, shaking themselves free of their defensive man. After the pass is made, the passer fakes toward the ball and cuts down the middle. The court should be kept balanced by having the cutter fill to the strong side. The team should attempt to keep the ball near the top of the circle. Each group is timed

to see which is able to control the ball for the longest period of time. Later in the drill layups are allowed if the team is able to control the ball past the 30-second mark.

Special Value of the Drill

It has been our observation over the past ten years that our most neglected fundamental is ball handling. We all know the importance and stress the fundamentals of individual defense, rebounding, and shooting, but somewhere in the daily practice plan something has to be squeezed out. It is obvious to us as we watch players come and go at all levels that ball handling is the assumed fundamental, the "black sheep" of the list. Yet nothing is prettier to watch than a team that can handle the ball. Every imporant fundamental in the game is included in this drill except shooting and rebounding. They can be added after the team has accomplished the major objectives of the drill. The basic goals for the drill include: timing, change of direction, court balance, individual defense, movement to get open as well as ball handling. After the drill is used for ten minutes, or to the satisfaction of the coach, the team can be rewarded by allowing a layup *after* the ball is controlled for at least 30 seconds. The poise and confidence gained by the squad through this drill can lead to many "no panic" finishes during the season, enjoyment of the followers, and, most important, smiles on the scoreboard at the conclusion of the contest.

Frank Truitt has been associated with teams that have posted a combined 362 wins and 139 defeats for a 72.2 winning percentage. His past includes three county league titles, a district crown, a regional title, a state runner-up, and an association with five Big 10 titles either won or shared. During his years as Ohio State assistant, he coached and helped develop Jerry Lucas and Gary Bradds, both collegiate Players-of-the-Year; John Havlicek, an All-American and All-NBA star; and pro players Larry Siegfried, Mel Nowell, and Joe Roberts.

FOUR-CORNER DRILL

Bobby Weise

Conroe High School, Conroe, Texas

The squad is divided into four equal numbers stationed in the corners of the floor. One line at each end has a ball. On command, X1 dribbles under control toward mid court with X2 in the other line breaking in the same direction. At about mid court X2 calls for the ball. X1 must be under control and make a good pass. X2 must take the ball on the move, gain

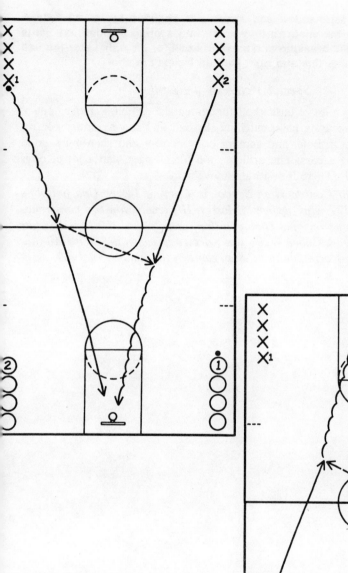

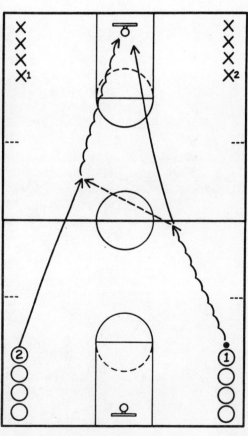

**control, dribble left-handed and shoot a left-handed layup. X1 follows
in and rebounds the shot. As they come into scoring position, O1 starts
his dribble with O2 breaking and making a call for the ball. Later the ball
is given to the other line and right-handed layups are shot.**

Special Value of the Drill

The drill involves a lot of basketball fundamentals: dribbling under control
and making an accurate pass, catching the ball and staying under control
while starting the dribble, and gaining body control and shooting a good
layup after taking a pass. The drill is good for all ages, and a lot of boys
can take part in it. There is continual movement.

*In five seasons at Conroe High School in Conroe, Texas, Coach Bobby
Weise recorded 127 wins against 33 losses. His teams won two conference
championships, one regional championship, and finished third in the state
tournament in 1968. Coach Weise was selected to coach the South All-Star
team in the State North-South All-Star game in the summer of 1969.*

3

Dribbling Drills

At one time in basketball, the dribble was considered a small man's art. This is no longer the case. Now, big men are also required to advance the ball by means of a dribble, change hands, and make quick starts and stops under control. Many offensive motions are initiated by means of the dribble and it can be used to set up teammates for shots. The fast break depends on the dribble, it is an effective technique to use in breaking the press, and it can be used as a means of ball control in the delay game. It is a popular skill with most players. Often they control the ball to excess and without good judgment; therefore, the skill and its proper use require much attention in practice.

FOUR-CORNER PASSING AND PIVOTING DRILL

Tay Baker

University of Cincinnati

The players form lines in each of the four corners in half court. The drill may be run with one ball, two balls diagonally, or four balls, one in each corner. #1 passes to #2 and gets a return pass half-way between the lines, running at full speed, taking the ball on into the corner on a dribble

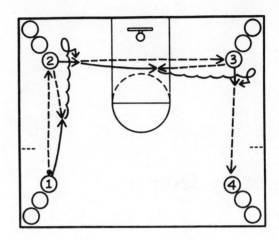

**if needed, using a pivot and handing the ball off to #2. The drill would
continue with #2 passing to #3, getting a return pass half-way between
the lines, taking the ball on into the corner, pivoting and handing off to
#3, etc.**

Special Value of the Drill

In addition to the obvious passing and pivoting values to be gained from
running the drill, it also serves as an excellent conditioner.

*A .700 winning percentage in a four-year schedule dominated by Missouri
Valley Conference teams and supplemented by many other major college
powerhouses (including one NCAA champion and an NIT titlist) is a tremendous coaching accomplishment, but that's the feat of Tay Baker, head
basketball coach at the University of Cincinnati. His four-year record
stands at 73–33. His first Bearcat quintet enjoyed a 21–7 record while
winning the Missouri Valley crown, got to the NCAA Midwest Regionals
(where elimination came in overtime to eventual national champ Texas-
El Paso), and ranked seventh and ninth in the final wire service polls. His
first year was also noteworthy in that he was named "Missouri Valley
Conference Coach of the Year" by his fellow coaches and by Associated
Press. In 1966–67 Baker's Bearcats went 17–9, including wins over MVC
champ Louisville and NCAA runner-up Dayton. The next year Cincinnati
finished 18–8 and claimed victories over MVC titlist Louisville, twice over
NIT king Dayton, and a triumph over Kansas State, the Big Eight winner.*

DEFENSIVE TRAILER DRILL

Bob Cope

Montana University

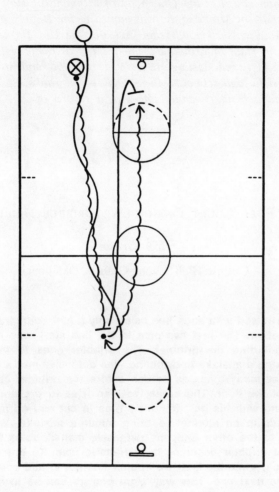

**The drill is used to give the players awareness of defensive pressure
from the rear when bringing the ball up court. The offensive player dribbles the ball up court at half speed. The defensive trailer attempts to
jab the ball away from him by moving from side to side. The defensive
trailer may not move farther than the offensive man's side. The offensive**

man changes dribbling hands to protect the ball. On the whistle the ball
is placed on the floor and offense becomes defense and defense, offense.
At this time a one-on-one situation occurs coming back to the end of the
court.

*After serving as assistant coach for three seasons, Bob Cope became the
head basketball coach at the University of Montana in 1968. A graduate
of the University of Montana, he was named to the Helm's Athletic Foundation All-America basketball team in 1948, the UM Basketball Hall of
Fame, and the State of Montana Athletic Hall of Fame. His career as a
head basketball coach, lasting from 1951 to 1965 and stretching from
coast to coast in high school, college, and service ranks, has brought him
to the Montana head coaching job with a record of 244 wins and 92
losses.*

FULL COURT ONE-ON-ONE DRIBBLE DRILL

Bob Griffin

Guthrie High School, Guthrie, Oklahoma

Two lines are used with each line using only a half court from one baseline to the other. The first two men in the line start, one dribbling and
the other guarding the dribbler. The dribbler goes to the other end
without making a mistake in dribbling. The defensive man's job is to turn
his dribble as many times as he can before the dribbler can get to the
other end of the floor. The defensive man tries to prevent the dribbler
from dribbling with his best hand. He tries to cut him off and make him
change hands in an attempt to bring about a mistake. When the two
players get to the other end, the defensive man dribbles the ball back
and the first dribbler becomes the defensive man. To get more players
going at once, when the first two in their line get to mid court, the coach
can start the next two. This way eight players can be in action at one
time.

Special Value of the Drill

This drill is an excellent conditioner. It teaches footwork on defense and
how to make a dribbler change directions. It teaches a boy to dribble with
either hand.

Bob Griffin coached at Guthrie High School in Guthrie, Oklahoma, for

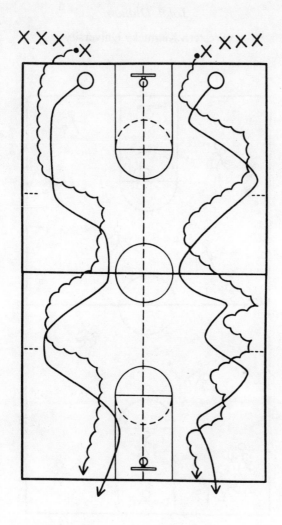

seven years, during which time he won 158 games and lost only 20. His teams went to the state playoffs six out of seven years. He won back-to-back state championships in the AA Classification during 1968 and 1969. His 1969 team had a perfect 24–0 record. He was named "Coach of the Year" in Oklahoma in 1960 and was the winning coach of the North All-Stars in the 1967 North-South All-Star Game in Oklahoma.

Towel Dribbling Drill

John Oldham

Western Kentucky University

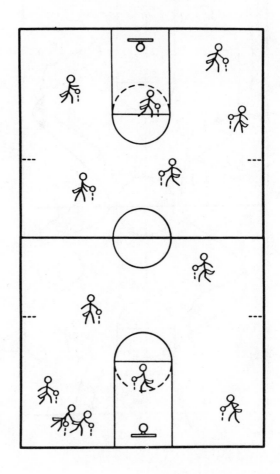

1. Coach blows his whistle and each player starts his dribble.
2. The dribbling players must steal the towel from another dribbling player. When a player loses his towel, that player is *out* of the drill.
3. Playing area is the basketball court.

Special Value of the Drill

1. Players learn to dribble with *head up!*
2. Great conditioner.
3. Fun in a fundamental (players really enjoy the drill).
4. When six players are left in the game, the area is restricted to half court.

The four seasons since Hilltopper Basketball Coach John Oldham became head mentor have been four of the most successful years in Western's long and illustrious basketball history. Coach Oldham's four-year record at Western includes: (1) two regular season OVC titles and one second-place finish; (2) four Holiday Tournament Championships; (3) three trips to national post-season tournaments; and (4) an overall record of 84 wins, 22 losses. Including his coaching record at Tennessee Tech before coming to Western, he has a lifetime collegiate win-loss record of 202–105 over a 13-year span.

PRESSURE DRIBBLING DRILL

Joe Ramsey

Robert Morris College

In this drill there are three lines with the players working in pairs. (X = offensive man; O = defensive man.) The offensive men dribble the ball in zig-zag motion (working on dribbling techniques), while the defensive men try to force the dribbler to change direction as often as possible. The offensive man will hesitate if he "beats" his defensive man until the defensive man gets back in position. When the dribbler reaches the far end of the court, the two men change assignments and the other man brings it back against pressure.

Special Value of the Drill

For teams that play pressure defense, this drill gets the defense accustomed to forcing the offense to go in the desired direction. Also, it demands that the dribblers use proper techniques and that they protect the ball when changing direction. Staying down in a defensive stance and dribbling against pressure are both great conditioners.

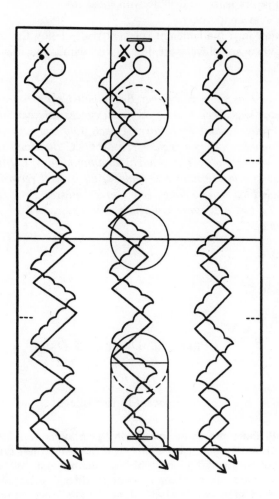

In his first four years of coaching, Joe Ramsey's teams have compiled a record of 112 wins against only 20 losses for a winning percentage of .849. As an assistant at Southern Illinois University for two seasons, he helped guide the teams to a 46–9 record. During this time they finished second in the NCAA College Division (1965–66) and won the NIT (1967). At Robert Morris College in his two years as head coach, he has compiled a 66–11 mark and led his teams to two Illinois State Championships. In 1967–68 his team finished eighth in the NJCAA Nationals, and in 1968–69 his team finished third.

Pass and Dribble Drill

Chuck Smith

University of Missouri at St. Louis

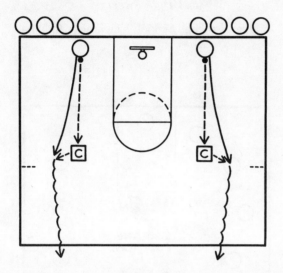

The player starts at the end line, passes the ball to the coach, and follows the pass. The coach drops the ball off to either side and the player on the run must pick up the ball, start his dribble and drive to the basket at the other end. The lines switch so the players can work with both hands.

Special Value of the Drill

It is an excellent drill for improving ball handling ability and quickness.

After a collegiate career as a guard at Washington University, Chuck Smith went into high school coaching and completed seven successful years at Leadwood and Bonne Terre, Missouri, High Schools, where his teams won approximately 70% of their games. In 1959 he returned to his alma mater as head basketball coach and accumulated an 84–59 record in six years at Washington University. In 1963–64 his team ranked ninth in the AP and UPI small college polls. Coach Smith left Washington University for the 1965–66 season to become head basketball coach at Central Missouri State College at Warrensburg, Missouri. In 1966 he accepted the head job at the University of Missouri at St. Louis. During the 1968–69 season his team participated in the NAIA tournament in Kansas City.

DRIBBLE TAG DRILL

Virgil Sweet

Valparaiso High School, Valparaiso, Indiana

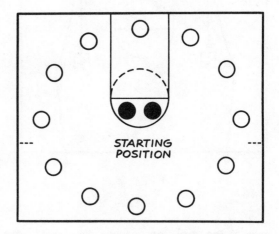

The drill requires half of a court and can utilize any number of players. All players have a ball and preferably wear dribble aids (blinders) to prevent them from watching the ball as they dribble. To start the drill, two players are in the middle and all other players are in a circle. The two middle players are "it" and must keep one hand above their head as they try to tag another player. The players in the circle may dribble anywhere on the half court to prevent being tagged. Once they are tagged, they raise their hand and become "it." There are two players trying to make the tag at all times.

Special Value of the Drill

1. The players must look up as they dribble to see the other dribblers.
2. Dribblers must use a full-speed dribble, change of pace, and various maneuvers to prevent being tagged.
3. The restricted area develops quickness in dribbling.

During 15 years as varsity basketball coach at Valparaiso High School in Valparaiso, Indiana, Virgil Sweet has won 12 Sectional Championships. His teams are widely known for their free throw shooting accuracy, having averaged over 70% from the line in each of the past 12 years. In addition to his coaching duties, Coach Sweet has written four basketball booklets and designed a plastic device for teaching dribbling called "Dribble Aids."

BIG MAN-LITTLE MAN DRIBBLING AND DEFENSE DRILL

Stan Watts

Brigham Young University

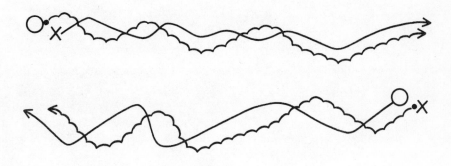

The big man dribbles with the little man defensing him. The little man then dribbles back with the big man defensing the little man. The play may be run either cross court or in a full court area.

Special Value of the Drill

This is an excellent drill for developing a big man's agility, speed, and movement. Using a little man with quickness offers a bigger challenge to the big man than working with someone his own size.

A generation spent with the Brigham Young varsity has netted Stan Watts and his teams two NIT championship trophies (1951 and 1966) and six conference championships, along with 385 victories to 224 defeats against some of the best competition in collegiate basketball. He began his coaching career at Millard High, where he was head coach in three sports. From Millard he moved to Dixie College as athletic director and basketball coach. He returned to the high school ranks in 1945 as head basketball coach at Jordan High. Two years later he joined the Brigham Young staff as an assistant coach. When the basketball post opened at that university in 1949, it was awarded to him.

4

Rebounding Drills

If passing and shooting are the heart of basketball, rebounding is the guts. Most coaches know its value and subscribe to the idea that games are won on the boards. Rebounding lacks glamour; only those players and coaches who work with it every day can fully appreciate the physical and mental toughness it requires. Timing, position, checking-out, and jumping ability are all factors to be emphasized in drillwork. The rewards to be gained will justify the effort.

"LEFT—RIGHT—STAY" REBOUNDING DRILL

Vince Budenholzer

Holbrook High School, Holbrook, Arizona

After the first pass by one of the three offensive players, the coach yells "Left," "Right," or "Stay." The defensive rebounders should then react accordingly to the left, or to the right, or stay and keep their man off the boards.

Special Value of the Drill

The drill helps teach rebounders to become aggressive in screening opponents off the boards. It also helps teach players to react to varying re-

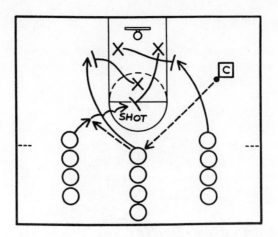

bounding situations, and improves timing and consciousness of the value of screening out.

In 13 years as a head coach and two years as an assistant, Vince Budenholzer has coached three state championships, one runner-up spot, one fourth, and seven conference championships. His lifetime win-loss record is 199 wins and 107 losses, including high school all-star victories in both New Mexico and Arizona.

THREE-MAN REBOUNDING WEAVE

Donald Clifton

Assistant Coach, Middle Tennessee State University

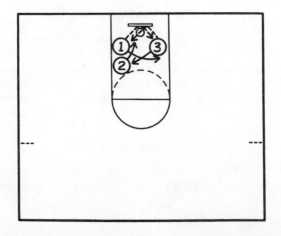

1. **The ball is always in the line where there are two players.**
2. **O1 shoots the ball on the center of the top of the square and changes lines quickly.**
3. **O3 rebounds the ball at its peak and follows the same procedure.**
4. **O2, in turn, rebounds the ball and follows the same procedure as the other two men.**

Each team of three players must successfully complete 25 consecutive rebounds before they can take a break. The ball must not touch the rim or hit the floor at any time. If it does, the threesome must begin again.

Special Value of the Drill

1. Great drill for timing.
2. Player must *focus* on center of square.
3. Helps develop spring.
4. Helps improve quickness and footwork.
5. Teaches teamwork.
6. Teaches the players to rebound at the peak of their jump.

Donald Clifton began his coaching career in 1965 at Mark Smith High School in Macon, Georgia. He served two seasons as the assistant basketball coach and two seasons as the head coach. His 1968–69 team won the State AAA Championship. During that season he was named Coach of the Year in Georgia and was selected to coach the South in the annual North-South All-Star Game. In four seasons at Mark Smith High his record was 70–24. He began a new post during the 1969–70 season as assistant coach at Middle Tennessee State University.

SPREAD EAGLE REBOUNDING DRILL

Bob Daniels

Kentucky Wesleyan College

Two men are put at the front of the circle. The man inside has the ball and the other man will be the offensive rebounder although he doesn't shoot. The other players are equally divided and lined up on the sideline. The inside man with the ball will throw the ball on the board and block out his man on the rebound. Once he has rebounded he turns to the side he is on and gets the outlet pass out quickly. The offensive rebounder then becomes the defensive rebounder and a man from the outlet lines will move out to become the offensive rebounder.

Special Value of the Drill

The rebounder gets practice under game-like conditions. He must block out well, go after the ball, and start the break. He is taught to snatch the ball off the boards, and shake his arms and hips in the offensive man's face. When he comes down he should exaggerate the spreading of his legs and arms. He should be immediately conscious of the outlet pass and should throw to the side he comes down on.

In two seasons as head coach at Kentucky Wesleyan, Bob Daniels won two straight NCAA College Division Basketball Championships. Enroute to the two championships, Daniels compiled 28–3 and 25–5 win-lost marks for a two-year record of 53–8! He came to Wesleyan in 1964. In his three years as assistant basketball coach, the Panthers won 59 of 81 games, including first and third place finishes in the NCCA Finals.

"MOUSE" REBOUNDING DRILL

Joe Edson

Brush High School, Brush, Colorado

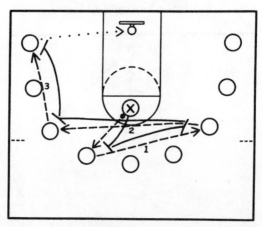

The players line up in a semicircle around the basket. One player is appointed as the "mouse," and goes on defense. He starts with the ball and follows the pass, playing tough defense on the man who has the ball. The ball must be passed three times before a shot can be taken. A pass cannot be made to a man next to the player with the ball. The player receiving the third pass shoots, and the "mouse" screens out the shooter and then goes to the board. If the defense gets the ball he makes a pass out to either X1 or X2, depending upon the direction of the rebound. If the offensive man gets the rebound, he continues to shoot until he scores or the defensive man gets the ball. When the defensive man rebounds and passes out, the offensive man who shot becomes the "mouse" and the defensive man takes his place in the semicircle.

Special Value of the Drill

This is a good drill for several reasons:

1. It teaches reaction and agility on the part of the defensive man.
2. It teaches the defensive man to box out the shooter.
3. It develops good rebounding habits.
4. Establishing the fastbreak with the pass to either X_1 or X_2 is also a benefit.
5. The offense benefits from making short passes and shooting under pressure. It teaches the offensive man to work to get position after a shot.

Joe Edson has coached at Brush High School in Brush, Colorado, for six years, during which time he has compiled 102 wins against 20 losses. His teams have been to the State AA Tournament five out of those six years, winning the consolation award once, fourth place, third place, and twice winning the State AA Championship. He was selected "Coach of the Year —AA" by the coaches in that class for the state of Colorado. He was also named coach of the North basketball team in the "AA-A" All-State North-South Basketball Game held in 1969.

OFFENSIVE REBOUNDING DRILL

Ed Fleener

Lincoln High School, Manitowoc, Wisconsin

1. O1 has the ball.
2. X1 is facing the basket, as is O1.
3. O1 shoots the ball.
4. O1 must step around X1 to recover the offensive rebound and score.

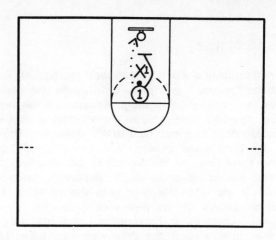

5. The drill should be done from a variety of angles.

   Note: 1. When the drill is first begun, O1 is instructed to slide around X1 to the right every time and then to the left every time.
   2. As the drill progresses, X1 is allowed to stop O1 as he tries to move around X1 for the offensive rebound.

Special Value of the Drill

1. Offensive rebounders can be taught not to give up when blocked off the boards by a defensive man.
2. The footwork technique of "spinning" and/or sliding around a defensive man is practiced by the offensive rebounder.
3. This drill can progress to a one-on-one offensive and defensive drill.
4. Timing and body positioning are very important.

From 1957 to 1965 Ed Fleener was assistant coach at Kirkwood, Rock Island, and Glen Ellyn schools in Illinois. In 1965 he became the head basketball coach at Lincoln High School in Manitowoc, Wisconsin. His four-year record at Lincoln is 74–17. His teams won two Fox Valley Conference Championships, three regional tournament championships, one sectional tournament title, and a state championship in 1968. His 1968 team was undefeated at 26–0. In 1967 he was named "Coach of the Year" in his conference.

THREE-MAN REBOUNDING DRILL

Dick Garibaldi

Santa Clara University

The squad is divided into three teams (with the players choosing the groups). The drill begins with the coach tossing the ball up on the board and the first player in each line attempting to rebound and put the ball

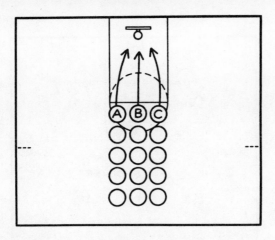

back up for a score. After a player has scored three times, he retires to the end of his line and the next man from that line hurries out to take his place. An individual player must remain in the rebound competition until he has scored three field goals. It is, of course, possible for one man (if he is small or lacks aggressiveness) to remain in the competition for a very long period of time. The first team to have all its members score three field goals is the winner. No fouls are called and there are no rules to prevent aggressive actions on the part of the individual.

Special Value of the Drill

This is a great drill for teaching competitiveness. It is a drill in which the bigger and less "skilled" player has an opportunity to find success. It can really stimulate a team to battle others and, at the same time, accustom the individual players to the rugged contact around the basket.

A former all-time basketball star at University of Santa Clara, Dick Garibaldi has completed his eighth season at the Bronco cage helm. During the 1967–68 and 1968–69 seasons he was honored as Northern California's "Coach of the Year" after guiding his Santa Clara quintet to two championships in the West Coast Athletic Conference with identical 13–1 records each season. Establishing many new Bronco team and individual records, Santa Clara raced to a 50–6 record during those two seasons. Prior to succeeding Bob Feerick as head Bronco mentor in 1962, Garibaldi coached the Santa Clara freshman team for four seasons.

BLOCKING OUT DRILL

Jim Hayes

B. B. Comer Memorial High School, Sylacauga, Alabama

In this rebound drill three men are on defense (O) and three men are on offense (X). The shooter stands at the top of the circle. When the ball is

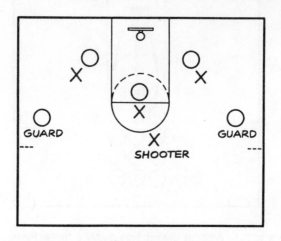

shot, the defense blocks out the offense and goes for the rebound. If the defense gets the ball, they make a quick outlet pass to their guards for the fast break. If the offense gets the ball, they try to put it back up for a goal. After the shooter has taken the shot he tries to intercept the pass out by the defense.

Special Value of the Drill

1. The defense works on blocking out and rebounding and making the quick pass to the guards.
2. The offense works on getting around the defense and putting the ball in the basket.
3. It is a competitive drill that is good for conditioning and toughness for the inside men.

Jim Hayes began his coaching career in Queen City, Texas, in 1956 where, during three seasons, he recorded 40 wins against 20 losses. In 1959 he moved to B. B. Comer Memorial High School in Sylacauga, Alabama. In ten seasons at Comer High, Coach Hayes has compiled a record of 179 wins and 80 losses. This record includes three invitational tournament championships, two conference championships, two regional championships, five area championships, four county championships, and one state championship (1968).

ONE-ON-ONE BLOCKING OUT DRILL

Dennis Huston

Clark College

The offensive man will shoot the ball and the defensive man will block off as both players go for the rebound. Whoever gets the ball (basket

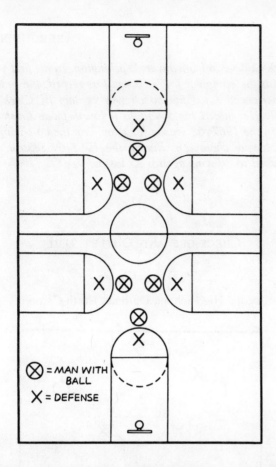

made or missed) will be the next shooter. The men usually position themselves in the area in which they operate on offense. The drill continues until the coach wishes to terminate it or to change player combinations.

Special Value of the Drill

In this drill the player is taught not to go immediately to the boards as the shot is taken. The defensive man learns to pause momentarily and let the shooter (who knows where the missed shot is going) make the first move. Then, he pivots on the foot in the direction in which the shooter moves. The defensive man makes contact with the shooter and then goes to the boards. This does two things: (1) it enables the player to get the long rebound (the one that often goes over the defensive man's head), and (2) it keeps the player between the ball and the shooter. Emphasis is placed not on holding the shooter back, but on just making contact momentarily and then going aggressively after the ball.

Dennis Huston began his coaching career at Camas Junior High School where he won 11 games while losing only one. After a year as an assistant coach at Western Washington State, he became the head basketball coach at Clark College in Vancouver, Washington. In his first year as coach of the Penguins, he compiled a 17–10 win-loss record, the best Clark College had experienced since the coach was captain of Clark's basketball team in 1961. He guided his squad to a fourth-place finish in the state tournament. In the 1967–68 season his team won the co-championship and then became league champions during the 1968–69 season, bringing his three-year record to 80 wins against 25 losses.

CHECK-OFF AND OUTLET DRILL

Doug Kistler

Jordan High School, Durham, North Carolina

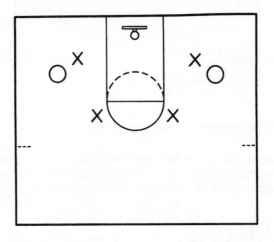

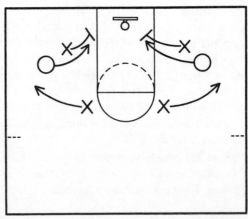

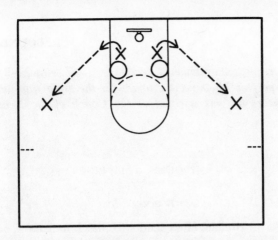

The purpose of the drill is threefold: (1) to provide practice in "checking-off"; (2) to provide an opportunity for aggressive rebounding; and (3) to breed an instinct for making the outlet passes. Personnel needed: 4 big men (forwards and centers) and 2 guards. STEPS: (1) The two guards station themselves at either side of the foul line. The offensive big men are free to move in the area from the baseline to the foul line extended. The defensive men must stay between their men and the basket. (2) The coach dribbles about the half court area—then shoots without warning. (3) The offensive players move toward the basket for the rebound and follow the shot. The defensive players must check off their opponent, being sure to keep him off his back. *Note:* The offense is allowed the liberty of "roughing up" the defense during the check-off and subsequent rebounding. This is a semi-controlled situation with no dirty play intended. (4) If the offensive player gets the rebound, he tries to put it back up. This is an opportunity for some one-on-one moves with the big men.

Note: If the offense makes the follow shot, the drill starts over again. (5) If the defensive player gets the rebound, he is immediately double-teamed and harassed by the opponents. But he must make an attempt to execute the outlet pass to the guard on his side. *Note:* When either defensive player gets the rebound, the guards move toward the sideline to receive the pass.

Special Value of the Drill

This drill is a valuable tool in determining which players can be counted on to pull down the "contested" rebound. The outlet pass is incorporated to help rebounders become aware of the importance of *looking* for the guard immediately after coming down with the rebound. When the drill is used regularly, rebounding totals go up.

After an outstanding playing career at Duke University, Doug Kistler became the head basketball coach at Jordan High School in Durham, North Carolina. In six years at Jordan High he recorded 104 wins against 33 losses. During this time he won three straight conference championships from 1966 to 1968. In 1966 his team placed fourth in the state tournament with a 21–4 record; they finished second in 1967 with 24–2; in 1968 his team had a perfect 26–0 record and won the state tournament. During these three years he was selected as the Coach of the Year in his conference.

FIGURE 8 TIPPING

Woody Neel

Holland High School, Holland, Indiana

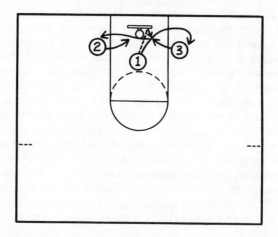

1 tosses the ball high off the board and moves in front of 3. 3 times the ball off the board and moves in and tips it up and over to 2. 3 moves in front of 2 and 2 tips the ball over to 1. This continues until the coach calls for the ball to be tipped in for the score.

Special Value of the Drill

This drill teaches the big men agility, timing, readiness, quickness of jumping, keeping the hands up, wrist and finger flick. It also has a value in conditioning. It's a good drill because it develops all the necessary rebounding skills.

In eight years of coaching, Woody Neel's teams won 12 championships and were tops in the state of Kentucky and Alabama. Coach Neel spent four seasons in Kentucky at Caneyville and Christian County high schools where he compiled 76 wins against 24 losses. His teams there won three district titles, one regional, one league, and one state runner-up title. In 1965 he became the head basketball coach at Holland High School in Indiana. Since that time he has recorded 78 wins against 14 losses and has won a Holiday Tournament, two sectional and two conference championships. His 1967–68 team was undefeated at 20–0.

THREE-ON-THREE REBOUNDING DRILL

Tony Nunes

De Anza College

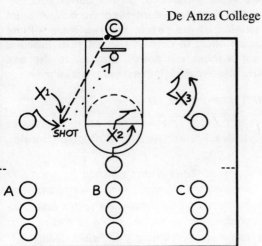

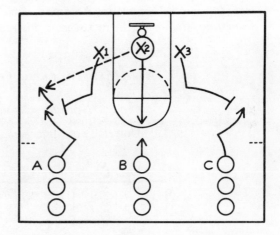

There are three players on defense (X) and three players on offense (O).
The coach will inbound the ball to one of the offensive players to start
the drill. After receiving the ball from the coach, the offense is allowed
no more than two passes before the shot is taken. Any one of the three
men may shoot. After the shot the three defensive men concentrate on
blocking out effectively. On a missed shot, if the defensive man rebounds
he must successfully outlet pass to one of the two pressured men at
the head of the three outside lines, A, B, and C. The pressure is provided
by the other two defensive men. If the shot is made, a defensive man
inbounds the ball to one of the two pressured men with the pressure
again being provided by his defensive teammates. Before the three de-

fensive men are finished they must score a total of ten points. A point is scored by the defense when they rebound and successfully outlet pass (or inbound successfully) to the new team of offensive men. They lose a point if they do not successfully inbound, do not outlet successfully, or commit any violation after they have controlled the ball. A point is also subtracted if, in the opinion of the coach, the two men without the ball do not make an adequate effort to contest the outlet or inbound pass. When the defensive team reaches ten points, they go to the end of the offensive lines and a new three-man defensive team takes over.

Special Value of the Drill

This drill gives the players an opportunity to work on all the defensive fundamentals under pressure. It teaches rebounding positions requiring tough physical contact.

After an outstanding career as a player, Tony Nunes coached for ten years at Sunnyvale High School in Sunnyvale, California, where his teams won 13 titles, four varsity and nine lightweight. His lightweight teams had winning streaks of 42 and 56, compiling an outstanding 128–6 record. His varsity teams were consistent contenders, winning 147 while losing 94. He spent the 1966–67 school year as an assistant coach at Foothill College. In 1967 he became the head basketball coach at De Anza College in Cupertino, California. In two seasons his record is 38–20.

FIVE-MAN BLOCKING OUT DRILL

Norman Olson

University of Minnesota at Duluth

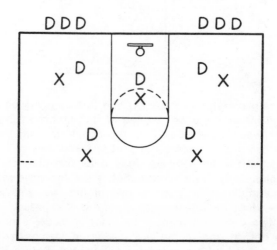

In this drill the block out is taught and practiced. The defense is rotated while the offensive men remain in position. Each defensive man gets the opportunity to block out a different man in a different position on the court. The reverse-pivot block out is taught after contact with the offensive man is made. Emphasis is placed on keeping the hands (rear of the hand) back. The drill is practiced each night because the success of every team rests upon its ability to block out and rebound effectively. This is the toughest teaching point on the team because of the skill's importance.

Special Value of the Drill

Even though the drill is simple, it is vital to a team's success. The players learn the value of position and develop aggressiveness and courage through its constant use.

In 28 years of coaching, Norman Olson has recorded 398 wins against 187 losses. In five seasons at Augusta High School his teams were 75–25. Following this, during eight years at Superior Central High School, he compiled a record of 85 wins and 35 losses. In 1954 he became the basketball coach at the University of Minnesota at Duluth. During 15 seasons his teams recorded 238 wins against 127 losses, including two NAIA titles. They were twice participants in NCAA Regional Tournaments.

TWO-ON-ONE DRILL

Daniel Peterson

Delaware University

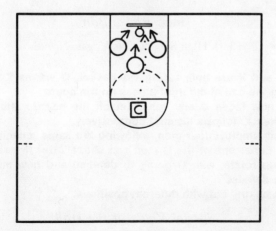

1. **Three men are in the offensive lane.**
2. **The coach shoots and misses.**
3. **The three men rebound aggressively.**
4. **The rebounder goes up for a three-point play.**
5. **The other two men aggressively try to stop the shooter.**
6. **The drill continues until someone scores.**
7. **The ball is then passed back to the coach. The ball is again shot and the drill is repeated.**

Special Value of the Drill

1. Develops poise on the offensive rebound thrust.
2. Develops the knack of making the three-point play.
3. Is an excellent conditioner.
4. Requires and teaches 2nd, 3rd, 4th, 5th, etc. efforts.

In 1962 Daniel Peterson became the assistant basketball coach at McKendree College under James "Barney" Oldfield. He moved to Michigan State University in 1963 to become freshman coach under Forrest Anderson. In 1965 he became plebe basketball coach at the U.S. Naval Academy under Ben Carnevale. He was named head basketball coach at the University of Delaware in May, 1966. In his first season, the Blue Hens compiled a 15–9 record. His 1967–68 team compiled a 16–7 record and won the Middle Five title with a 7–1 record. The Blue Hens were 11–10 in 1968–69, boosting his three-year record to 42–26.

SPECIAL REBOUNDING DRILL

Jack Richardson

Clark High School, Las Vegas, Nevada

Phase 1. **O and X are both facing the basket. O warms X up by throwing the ball at different places on the board.**

Phase 2. **X now faces O and rolls him off the boards after the shot is taken. O follows his shot aggressively.**

Phase 3. **This employs four men, following the same technique as phase 2. Either one of the O men can shoot. After five repetitions the men rotate, with O going to defense and new men coming in on defense.**

Phase 4. **Same drill but with different positions.**

Special Value of the Drill

Rebounding drills have always been a problem. Most coaches avoid any special drills for rebounding and we were doing the same until we devised

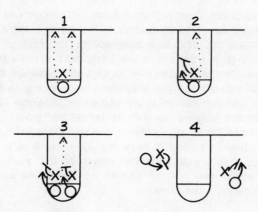

this drill. It allows the players to work on rolling out, positioning, re-bounding, lateral movement, and avoiding being screened off the boards.

Jack Richardson began his coaching career in 1963 at Hyde Park Junior High School in Las Vegas where in one season he recorded 18 wins and two losses. The next season he moved to Garside Junior High and won 16 games while losing four. In 1965 he became the head basketball coach at Clark High School in Las Vegas. During four seasons he has compiled a record of 70 wins and 17 losses. During the 1967–68 and the 1968–69 seasons his teams won the Nevada AA State Championship.

CHECK OUT—THROW OUT DRILL

James Snyder
Ohio University

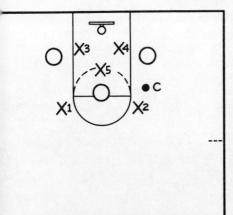

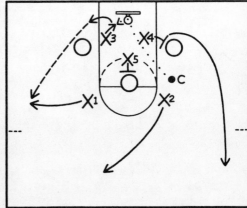

Men are placed in defensive, check out positions (forwards and centers are normally used in the 3-4-5 spots). Offensive men are placed in their positions on the court. Guards 1 and 2 are left uncovered. A coach with the ball will stand about 15-20 feet from the basket. He shoots to miss. Rebounders check out first and then go for the ball. A great deal of stress on the check out occurs in the early part of the season. If X3 rebounds, he turns to the outside and throws the baseball pass to X1. As soon as X1, X2, and X4 see the side the ball is going to be rebounded, they anticipate and release to spots shown in Diagram #2. In the early part of the drill the players go only as far as half court. By keeping at half court, time can be saved—players can get more rebounds and more throw outs in a limited period of time. If players were to break the whole way each time, they would lose the effect of the start of this break. This way, the stress can first be placed on the check out, then on the throw out and finally on the release.

Special Value of the Drill

Rebounding is a major part of winning. Great emphasis must be given this part of the game. Check out can be heavily stressed but it does not necessarily lend itself to good fast breaking. This drill is very game-like, including all elements necessary in good fast breaking.

James Snyder has been basketball coach at Ohio University (Athens) since the 1949–50 season. As dean of the Mid-American Conference coaches, his overall record at Ohio is 270–201, and he has won four MAC titles (1960, 1961, 1964, 1967). His teams have appeared in four NCAA Tournaments and one NIT Tournament. His 1963–64 team advanced the farthest of any MAC team in the NCAA district playoffs, defeating Louisville in the sub-regionals, then downing Kentucky in the first round of the Mideast Regional competition. Before assuming the head job at Ohio University, Coach Snyder coached the freshman team at Ohio University for three seasons.

5

Individual Ability Development Drills

Basketball is one of the most complex sports ever devised. It requires a high degree of skill in a number of areas. Running, jumping, throwing, passing, and shooting are coordinated in a smoothly flowing sequence. Much time must be devoted to the development of these individual skills.

JUMPING DRILLS

Bob Calihan

University of Detroit

One Man Drill

1. Jump up and touch the rim ten times or come as close to the rim as possible.
2. Jump and tip the ball off the *right* side of the backboard ten times, using the right hand.
3. Jump and tip the ball off the *left* side of the backboard ten times, using the left hand.
4. While standing on one side of the basket, jump and push the ball with two hands high over the basket to the other side. Move over quickly, jump, and recover the ball. Repeat back and forth, recovering the ball at least ten times.

Two Man Drill

5. With one player on each side of the basket, jump and push the ball with two hands back and forth at an angle off the backboard. Repeat the maneuver ten times and then reverse positions for another ten jumps. This drill should be executed without catching the ball and bringing it down. Jump, catch, and push the ball back before the feet touch the floor.

6. With a teammate, repeat the last drill but catch the ball, come down, and then go up and push the ball back across the backboard. Repeat this maneuver ten times and then reverse positions for another ten jumps.

After each series the player will shoot two free throws, which makes for game-like conditions.

Special Value of the Drill

Second in importance to running is jumping. Skilled jumping will improve rebounding. Strong rebounding will win basketball games. This is a daily drill to improve individual rebounding. It also aids in timing and fingertip control of the ball.

Already the winningest basketball coach in the school's history with 303 victories, Bob Calihan is also in his sixth year as the Director of Athletics for his alma mater. His best seasons have been 1949–50 when the Titans were 20–6; the Dave DeBusschere era (1960–61–62) when Detroit earned bids to post-season tournaments; and 1964–65 when it won 20 games and returned to the NIT. Detroit played in the 1960 and 1961 National Invitation Tournaments and the 1962 NCAA Championships. The Titans had winning years in 16 of Calihan's 21 seasons.

ALL-PURPOSE DRILL—INDIVIDUAL DEVELOPMENT

Jack Gardner
University of Utah

Two players work together. One dribbles forward for approximately 15 feet, makes a stride stop and pivot while protecting the ball from an imaginary defensive man. The second player times himself while following the dribbler so he can fake (to set up a defensive man) and receive a short flip pass from the player who just pivoted. The second player then dribbles forward approximately 15 feet, completes a stride stop and pivot, and passes off to the player coming to receive the pass. This pattern continues to the end of the playing floor and then is repeated back to the original beginning point.

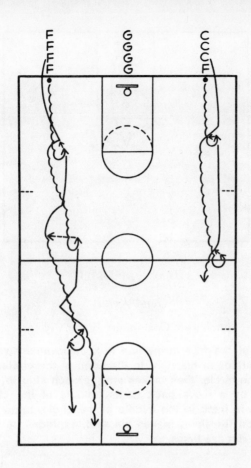

Special Value of the Drill

This is called our all-purpose drill since we try to teach dribbling, stride stops, pivots, ball protection, short passes (protected by body), timing to follow a dribbler, fake to set up a defensive man, and position to receive a pass with balance and timing to stop if a jump switch should occur.

Jack Gardner has been the head coach at the University of Utah since 1953. During this time he has established a record that is comparable to that of any coach in the nation. In fact, from 1953 to 1969 he has won 306 games, almost 20 per season. He is one of only a few coaches to take his squads to the final round of the NCAA Championships four times. In 30 years of coaching, his teams have won 15 championships. At Utah, he has won seven titles in 15 years, and his career win-loss percentage is well above the 70% mark. The affable strategist is listed number six in the nation's top 20 basketball coaches. At a recent meeting of the National Association of Basketball Coaches in Los Angeles, Jack Gardner received two awards from his peers. He was presented with the organization's Award of Merit and the Honor Award for his outstanding contributions to collegiate basketball.

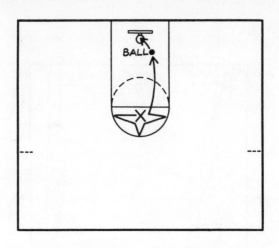

REACTION DRILL

Gene Keady

Hutchinson Community Junior College

A player starts at the free throw line in a basic defensive position. On command he shuffles to his right to the edge of the circle, then back to the middle of the circle, then makes an approach step to the top of the circle followed by a move back to the middle of the circle. He then shuffles to his left, back to the middle of the circle, turns around, grabs the basketball on the floor, makes his shot, explodes up after the shot and touches the rim five times.

Special Value of the Drill

The drill is an excellent early-season conditioner which teaches good fundamental movement. The player must learn to go at top speed but under control.

In his first three seasons as head basketball coach at Hutchinson Junior College, Gene Keady compiled an impressive record of 64 wins against only 18 losses, while winning the Kansas Junior College Championship twice. Coach Keady came to Hutchinson in 1965 as an assistant coach and took over the reins in 1966. Before this he coached at Beloit and brought teams to the Class A State Tourney three times.

INDIVIDUAL OFFENSIVE MOVES

Howie Landa

Mercer County Community College

A great emphasis must be placed on offensive basketball. A player feels that the coach is showing confidence in him when he is given one-on-one

98

practice. We work on our one-on-one moves every day for 15 to 20 minutes. These moves in particular are given attention and we expect our players to develop the ability to use each effectively.

1. Rocker step, move back, for the one-hand, jump, or set shot.
2. Fake and drive right all the way for the layup.
3. Fake and drive right all the way to the basket, stop, and go up strong.
4. Fake and drive right, go under the basket and to the other side of it. Use the right hand and go up with the right leg.
5. Fake and drive right, go to the other side of the basket, use the left hand, and go up with the left leg. A left-handed hook shot is taken.
6. Fake and drive right. Stop for a quick jump shot.
7. Fake and drive right. If the defense will not permit a drive to the baseline, a whirl-back movement is made. The reverse pivot precedes a left-handed hook shot.
8. Fake right with the right foot and then drive left and to the middle for a jump shot.
9. Fake right with the right foot and drive left for a layup shot, shooting with the left hand.
10. All moves are made on the other side of the court with the opposite hand.

Howie Landa began his coaching career at Shamokin (Pennsylvania) High School where he recorded 65 wins against only eight losses for three straight district championships. In 1961 he moved to Neshaminy (Pennsylvania) High School and notched 17 wins against eight losses. He coached the suburban Philadelphia All-Stars during that season. In 1962 he accepted the head job at Trenton Junior College in Trenton, New Jersey. During his years at Trenton, Coach Landa's record is 151–53. His teams have won the Region XV title twice, finished sixth in the nation (1963–64), and 11th in the nation (1966–67). He was Coach of the Year in 1968 in the NJCAA.

Four-step Individual Drills

Frank La Porte

Bishop O'Dowd High School, Oakland, Cal.

Stick Shift Move—Player dribbles with right hand from right side toward a chair, uses a stick shift movement with the ball when he approaches the center of the chair, and "shifts from second to third gear." Then he goes around chair to the basket or shoots a quick jump shot.

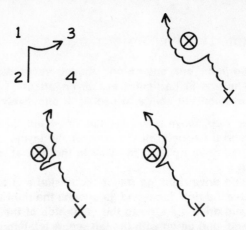

Cross Over Drill—The player dribbles with his right hand from the right side toward a chair. As he approaches the chair he uses a cross dribble to the left of the chair, making sure that the right leg cuts the defensive man off, and then he drives to the basket with the left hand.

Cross Over and Reverse—The player follows the same procedure as he did in the cross over drill but now, instead of continuing to drive to the basket, the player reverses direction by bringing the ball back with his left hand.

Fake Reverse—Again the player dribbles toward the chair with the right hand, but now he fakes a spin around a defensive man but turns his body only ¼ turn and then continues forward, similar to a rocker-step.

Special Value of the Drill

This drill is very effective in teaching individual moves and ball handling. It is also switched to the left hand.

In 11 seasons at Bishop O'Dowd High School in Oakland, California, Frank La Porte has compiled an enviable 312–65 overall record with a commendable array of tournament victories, and has produced four All-American basketball players during his coaching career at Bishop O'Dowd. In 1962 and 1967 he was honored as the East Bay Prep Writers "Coach of the Year," and also in 1967 in recognition of his fine record he was honored "All-Northern California Coach of the Year." In 1967 the O'Dowd Dragons were the number one team in the State of California with a record of 37–2.

ALL-PURPOSE DRILL

Andy Locatelli

Santa Barbara City College

The players form a line in the area of mid-court on the right side. The first player begins the drill by dribbling toward the baseline with his

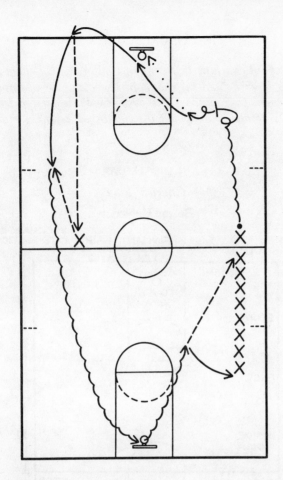

right hand. He switch dribbles when he reaches the free throw line extended, and executes a jump stop facing the left sideline. He now uses a rear turn with his right foot as the pivot foot and comes back around in a balanced position for a jump shot. He follows the shot and gets his own rebound. After the rebound he steps out of bounds and baseball passes to a man at mid-court, follows the pass, and receives a return pass. After receiving the ball he dribbles to the other end of the court for a layup. He gets his own rebound and dribbles to the mid-court area where he stops and passes to the next man in the line. Several balls may be used in the drill.

Special Value of the Drill

This is an excellent all-purpose drill utilizing many fundamentals: dribbling, switching, stopping, pivoting, jump shooting, offensive rebounding, baseball passing, cutting, and layup. It can be used from either side with many variations.

In 1969 Andy Locatelli became the head basketball coach at Santa Barbara City College in Santa Barbara, California, after 11 years of very suc-

cessful high school coaching in Northern California. He spent five seasons at St. Francis High School in Mountain View and six seasons at Willow Glen High School in San Jose. His 1968–69 Willow Glen team was undefeated at 27–0 and was named the number 1 team in Northern California.

LINE DRILL

Charles Luce

Boston University

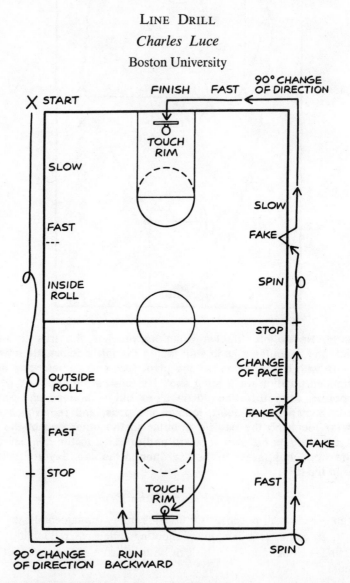

Using the lines of the court, the player always runs in one direction but makes moves that are made in a game. This can be used as a follow-the-leader type drill as well as an individual drill.

Special Value of the Drill

This drill serves as a conditioner, but at the same time gives the player work on many of the types of action that he must use in a game. He gets a lot of work on many things in a short period of time. This drill is especially good for the big man.

During his tenure at Dobbs Ferry High School, from 1953 to 1957, Charles Luce's teams won five basketball championships, and one was selected as the outstanding team in the area. He was personally honored by being named "Coach of the Year" on two occasions. In 1957 he moved to Greenwich High where he transformed a team that had only one winning team in ten years into a winner. In 14 years of high school coaching, he had teams that rolled up an overall record of 201 wins and 69 losses. In 1967 he accepted the head post at Boston University.

DRIBBLE DRIVE DRILL

Doug Schakel

Lamar High School, Lamar, Colorado

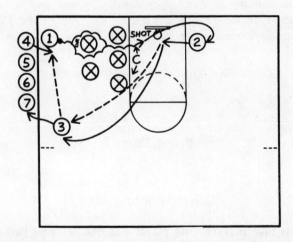

1 starts the drill by driving toward and weaving through the football dummies (spaced approximately three feet apart—the first line of dummies is about eight-ten feet from second line of dummies) in an attempt to score on a close-in shot. The coach is stationed behind the center dummy and he tries to bother 1 as he passes through one of the two holes. A hand is put in 1's face as he is attempting the shot. At first this is very disconcerting to the shooter but after a while he regains his con-

centration. If 1 is not protecting the ball as he slides through the hole an attempt is made to slap it away—otherwise the ball is left alone.

About halfway through the drill the coach will change his assignment by jumping into one of the holes just after 1 passes the first line of dummies. This forces the dribbler to control his drive and avoid the offensive charge foul. 1 can either pull up and shoot the short jumper or change direction and drive through the unoccupied hole to the basket.

2 rebounds 1's shot, passes to 3 and follows his pass. 3 passes to 4 who drives through the dummies. 3 goes to the end of the line. When the dribbler drives through the hole farther from the basket, the flash hook is encouraged. The dribbler may pick any route he chooses as he drives in and around the dummies.

Special Value of the Drill

The drill is good for three reasons: (1) it reduces the number of offensive fouls on the baseline drive; (2) it increases the success of a shot in a congested area; and (3) it gives players good dribbling practice and teaches them to keep their heads up.

Doug Schakel began his coaching career in 1964 at Central College (Iowa) where he was the frosh coach. After a year at Solon High School in Iowa he came to Crowley County High School in Ordway, Colorado, where he spent three very successful seasons. From 1966 through 1968 his teams won 60 games while losing only 11. In 1966 his team was the AA State consolation runner-up; in 1967 they finished third; and in 1968 they were AA State Champions with a perfect 24–0 record. In 1969 Coach Schakel began his first season at Lamar High School in Lamar, Colorado.

Pivot Drill

Prentice Waller

University of Arkansas

This drill uses four players. One player has the ball and two others are doing everything they can to tie up the boy with the ball or get it from him. This forces the player with the ball to pivot and protect the ball. At the same time, the fourth boy is moving around and trying to stay out of his sight. Now, while pivoting and protecting the ball, the player being trapped must find the free player. He must pivot and protect the ball for at least five seconds before he is allowed to pass off. After the player passes out of the trap, the two players pursue and trap the boy who received the pass. After two or three minutes the teams are changed.

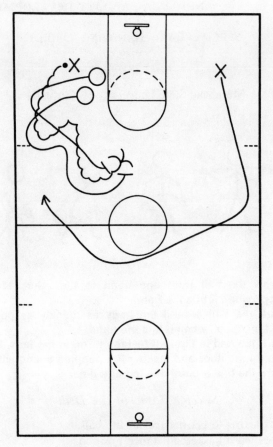

Special Value of the Drill

This drill has been of great help in learning to handle the many traps encountered in pressure defenses. It also gives practice in dribbling and passing.

When Glen Rose retired in 1967, Prentice (Duddy) Waller was rewarded with the head basketball post at the University of Arkansas. He had ably assisted Rose over a nine-year span, during which time he coached freshman basketball teams to a record of 74–32. He entered the high school coaching ranks as soon as he received his degree from the University of Arkansas—first at Camden Fairview for one year where his record was 20–7, then on to Stephens High School for two years where he recorded 44 wins against 17 losses. From there he went to Southern State as head coach for three years and finished with a 28–6 record that earned the Muleriders an NAIA berth. That's when he was invited to join the Razorback staff. Add his 64–24 high school record to his frosh record of 74–32, and a five-year college mark of 77–50, and Waller has a life-time mark of 215–106 (.669).

Special Ball Handling Drills

Bob Wright
Morehead State University of Kentucky

Figure 1. Throw the ball from one hand to the other. Make the ball "pop" when it hits the hand.

Figure 2. Work the ball around the body as quickly as possible. Make the ball "pop" when it hits the hand.

Figure 3. Work the ball in figure 8 fashion through the legs, keeping both feet on the floor and making the popping sound with the hands.

Figure 4. Work the ball around one leg at a time.

Special Value of the Drill

1. Player learns to get the feel of the ball.
2. Players learn basketball stance position.
3. Strengthens the wrist and lower arm.
4. Teaches the player to keep his head up.
5. Good conditioning drill when movement is combined with the ball handling.

Before coming to Morehead State, Bob Wright spent 13 years on the high school level where he compiled a 329–72 record. At Ashland High School he led the Tomcats to 168 wins and only 29 defeats and was named Kentucky "Coach of the Year," with his team winning the state championship in 1961. During his four years at Morehead State, his record is 58–38. This represents one tie for the championship of the Ohio Valley Conference and a second, third, and fourth place finish. In 17 years of coaching he has never had a losing season in basketball.

6

Conditioning Drills

The objective of conditioning drills should be to increase the players' endurance and stamina through extended physical activity. Strength and durability must be built during the off-season. A conditioning program should be an important part of the total organizational plan, and should be designated to produce in each individual a state of readiness to endure the many physical challenges he will face.

LINE CONDITIONING DRILL

Dan Ayala

Pasadena City College

Combine teams into two groups (all big men and all little men, or all guards and all centers and forwards). Race starts on the whistle behind the 0 line. Each man must touch the 1 line and return and touch the 0 line; then back to the 2 line and return to the 0 line; then on to the 3 line and back to the 0 line; touch 4 and back to 0; touch 5 and back to 0; touch 6 and back to 1. 1 is the finish line. This allows a stopping distance to prevent stopping too suddenly. Give two points to winner and one point to second place. A player must accumulate four points to stop. As each man accumulates four points, he stops. Everyone runs until he accumulates four points. While one group dribbles, the other group rests.

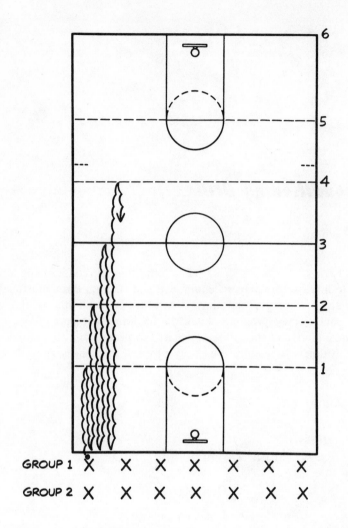

GROUP 1 X X X X X X X

GROUP 2 X X X X X X X

Special Value of the Drill

In addition to being a great conditioner, the drill gives players practice in starting, stopping, body balance, and dribbling.

Dan Ayala began his coaching career at Beaumont High School, where he compiled a 48–22 record while leading his teams to one championship and two second-place finishes. From there he moved to Mt. San Jacinto College where his teams won two championships and finished in second place once. While at Mt. San Jacinto College he recorded 55 wins against 18 losses. In 1969, his first season at Pasadena City College, his team was 27–5, winning its league title and going on to become state JC champions.

"SUICIDE" CONDITIONING DRILL

Al Bianchi

Washington Capitols

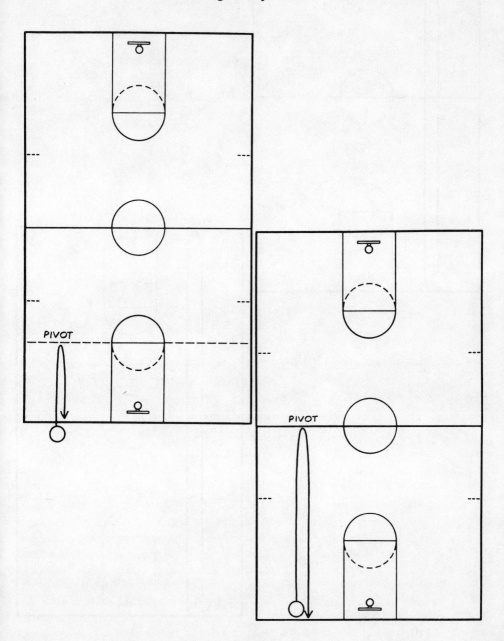

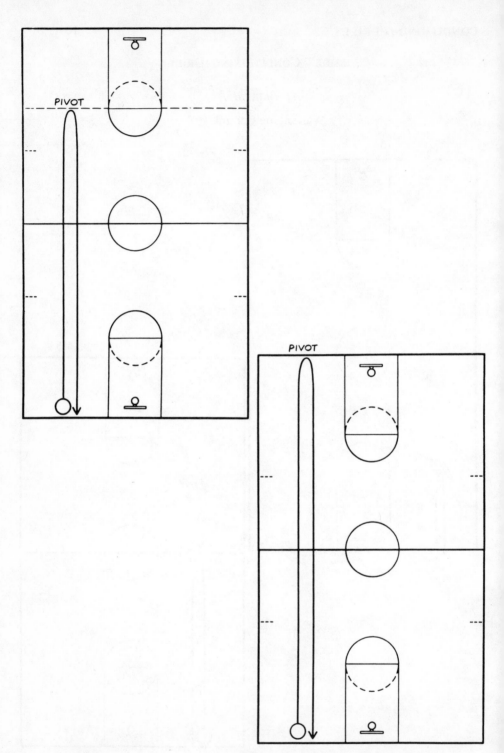

1. **Players are lined up along the end line. Big men and little men are separated.**
2. **The coach gives the starting signal with a whistle. The players must run and touch an imaginary free throw line extended, then back to the end line.**
3. **They then run to center line and back to the end line.**
4. **Players then run to imaginary free throw line extended at the opposite end of the court and back to the end line.**
5. **The drill is completed when the players run to the opposite end line and back.**

Special Value of the Drill

This drill is usually run after practice or just before shooting free throws. It is most beneficial when players are tired. It makes them push themselves, which is the best way to get in shape. Players hate it—coaches love it!

After a year with the Seattle Supersonics, Al Bianchi recently took over the Washington Caps in the American Basketball Association. Already known as one of the outstanding young coaches in the National Basketball Association, he provided an exciting, competitive team in the Sonics' first year of operation and displayed an amazing knack of getting the best possible performances out of his athletes. In his ten seasons as a player and one campaign as assistant coach to John Kerr at Chicago, Bianchi had never failed to be in action at playoff time. He attended Bowling Green University in Ohio, and in his senior year was the nation's ninth leading collegiate scorer. He was drafted on the second round by the Minneapolis Lakers and later went to Syracuse. Bianchi played in 687 regular season games during his career, scoring 5,561 points for an average of 8.1 per contest.

Sliding Defensive Drill

John Dromo

University of Louisville

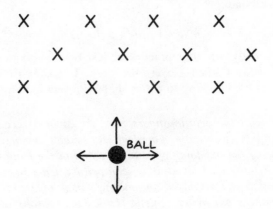

Players start with three minutes and work up to ten minutes a day. The ball is dribbled any way and the defensive men, in correct stance, slide with the ball. The players are allowed to use a boxer's crouch or a wrestler's crouch.

Special Value of the Drill

Defense is the name of the game. When your hands go down, you are beat. Players must learn to stay low *all* the time. This drill builds up muscles and saves on other phases of conditioning. Sometimes a towel is put around the player's neck and he has to hold the towel with both hands.

John Dromo took over as head basketball coach in 1967 after serving a 19-year apprenticeship as the assistant coach at the University of Louisville. His frosh clubs won 233 of 268 outings during that period. But it was in the field of recruiting that Dromo won national stature. The peak was reached in 1964 and 1965 when he corralled first Westley Unseld and then Butch Beard, the two top prospects of that period in Kentucky. Since taking the head job, he has recorded 41 wins against 13 losses. In 1967–68 his team was the Missouri Valley Conference champion, and in 1968–69 Louisville was the MVC co-champion.

INDOOR-OUTDOOR CONDITIONING DRILLS

Ernest Fears

Norfolk State College

The conditioning drills are divided into two classes: (1) out-of-doors and (2) in-doors.

Outdoors

1. *Burma Road.* The players line up along the goal line on the football field. They are given three blows of the whistle: (1) first whistle=trot 20 yards; (2) second whistle=fast trot 20 yards; (3) third whistle=sprint 20 yards. This is done for five minutes.
2. *Goal Post Jump.* The coach stands next to the goal post and gives the command, "Jump." The players jump, and touch the cross bar. This is repeated 15 times. On the 15th time the player sprints back to the cross bar and repeats drill. This is done four times.
3. *Stomach Roll.* Players get on their stomachs with their hands and arms extended. They merely roll the length of the field (100 yards).

Indoors

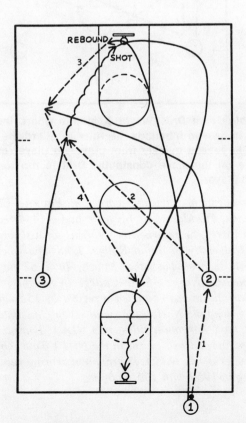

1. *Big Man Drill.* O1 passes in to O2. O2 passes to O3 going in for a layup. O1, after passing to O2, must be down court to take the ball off the board and shoot if the layup is not made. If the basket is made, he takes it out of bounds and passes to O2 who has moved down court into the outlet area on the opposite side from which he started. After receiving the pass from O1, O2 again passes to O3. This is repeated six times.

2. *Give-and-Go Drill.* Players simply pass the ball back and forth as they move down the court. This is repeated six times.

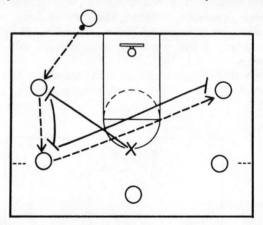

3. *Double Team Drill.* Player X stands where indicated and when ball is passed inbounds, he runs to guard the ball handler. The ball is passed quickly from player to player so that X will have to be on the move constantly. Drill is run for one minute with each player.

Ernest Fears began his coaching career at Blanche Ely High School in Pompano Beach, Florida, where his team had a 14–4 record. After serving in the armed forces, he returned in 1956 as an assistant basketball coach at Southern University in Baton Rouge, Louisiana where in 1958 he accepted the job as head basketball coach. In 1962 he became the head basketball coach at Norfolk State College in Norfolk, Virginia. In seven seasons at Norfolk he has compiled a record of 152 wins against only 31 losses. During this time Norfolk has won seven Christmas Holiday Tournaments, two CIAA Visitation titles, two CIAA Tournaments, one district championship, and finished fourth in the NAIA Tournament in 1965. Norfolk is the holder of six NAIA Tournament scoring records. It led the nation in scoring in 1969 with 106.1 points.

FIVE-MAN FIGURE 8 DRILL

Grant Gray

West Virginia State College

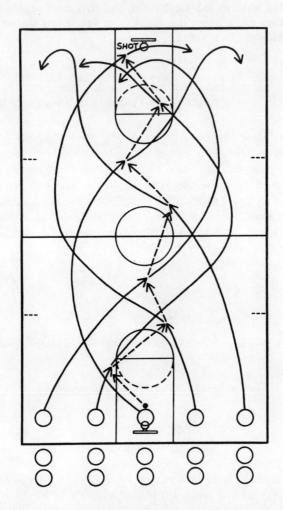

**The squad is divided into five separate groups. Each group forms a line.
The first member of each of the groups participates in the drill. The five
front men are lined up along the baseline facing the opposite basket.
One man is directly under the basket, with two men on each side of him.
As the five front men of each line start the drill, the players who are
second in line now assume the front of the line. At the successful conclusion of the drill the participants move to the rear of the line. This is a**

pass and cut drill with the passer always following his pass to the out-side and behind two men. The first pass is always made by the middle man of the five players. The receiver is the near man on either side. The ball should always be progressed up court with a pass. Dribbling is not allowed. The five men progress up court and return, using the pass and cut. They shoot a layup as they reach the basket at each end of the court. After the shot at the far basket, the five men reassemble in five lanes and return back down the court. The five lanes should be spaced equally from sideline to sideline.

Special Value of the Drill

In addition to being a great conditioning drill, it also provides the players with practice in passing, cutting, and filling the lanes properly as a co-ordinated unit.

Grant Gray became the head coach of the West Virginia State Yellow Jackets during the 1967–68 season. Prior to this his coaching experience includes three years at Tillotson College (Austin, Texas) and four years at Prairie View A & M University (Prairie View, Texas) as head basketball coach. In 1954 he came to West Virginia State College as basketball coach of the now vanished state high school. There he served as assistant football coach for ten years, head baseball coach, and assistant basketball coach to the late Mark H. Cardwell for 12 years.

INDIVIDUAL BASKETBALL EXERCISES

Dr. Fred Lewis

Sacramento State College

After an outstanding career as a player, Fred Lewis moved into the coach-ing ranks by accepting a position at Amityville (New York) High School for four years. In 1954 he went to the University of Hawaii as assistant basketball coach. After Hawaii he spent a year at Southern Illinois as an assistant coach. He then accepted the head job at Mississippi Southern in 1957. In five years his quintets won 88 games and lost just 38, and in one stretch ran off a 26-game winning skein. In 1962 he accepted the post at

EXER-GENIE® EXERCISER

Efficiency in Exercise

INDIVIDUAL BASKETBALL EXERCISES

By DR. FRED LEWIS

① BIG FOUR—22 seconds
(Deadlift-Clean-Military Press)

GENERAL INSTRUCTIONS

Always begin each exercise period with easy bending and stretching. The following workout should take from 10-30 minutes. The degree of work should depend primarily on the initial strength of the individual. As strength increases, the intensity of the workout should also increase.

All exercises should be done using one repetition and should be continued throughout the season.

Sufficient resistance should be set to insure maximum effort throughout the entire workout. Correct form should be maintained while following the newly applied principle of exercising isometrically for ten seconds and then without relaxing moving to the isotonic (movement) phase of the exercise, working at maximum resistance throughout the exercise. If the 'buddy system' is used, see exercises on opposite page.

On all exercises the trail line should be controlled with the index finger so line will not move during the ten second isometric contraction. Setting of the exerciser will vary with each exercise and each individual. It should take not more than 22 seconds to complete the exercise. Start each exercise with a ten second isometric contraction and then move through a full range of motion within twelve seconds.

Set resistance for maximum performance of the Clean. Use rowing handle—anchor unit to footboard. Stand on footboard with feet apart. Assume Deadlift position as illustrated above. Hold ten second isometric contraction, controlling trail line with index finger and pull straight up with maximum effort, keeping arms straight until legs have raised body to erect position. Release trail line slowly for maximum resistance while straightening legs (Deadlift - 4 seconds.) Without relaxing, release trail line, moving hands to chin (Clean - 4 seconds.) Without relaxing, rotate hands, palms outward, moving handle above head as far as possible, while stretching and rising to toe raise (Military Press - 4 seconds.)

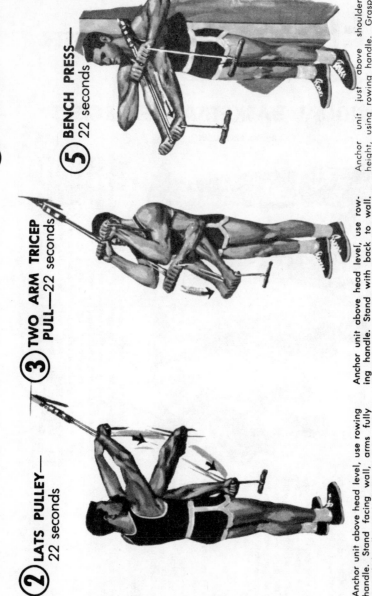

④ REPEAT BIG FOUR

⑤ BENCH PRESS— 22 seconds

Anchor unit just above shoulder height, using rowing handle. Grasp handle, elbows in Bench Press position, as illustrated. Hold 10 second isometric contraction, pushing to maximum against handle. Release trail line and without relaxing, push handle forward, extending arms away from body. (12 seconds).

③ TWO ARM TRICEP PULL—22 seconds

Anchor unit above head level, use rowing handle. Stand with back to wall. Grasp handle, hold at top of head, elbows in tight. Exert maximum isometric contraction for 10 seconds. Release trail line. Keeping elbows at 45 degree angle, move immediately through range of motion until elbows at sides. Extend arms out straight and down to waist position.

② LATS PULLEY— 22 seconds

Anchor unit above head level, use rowing handle. Stand facing wall, arms fully extended, elbows locked. Grasp handle and exert maximum downward isometric contraction for 10 seconds. Without relaxing release trail line, move handle down across front of body to waist position, keeping arms fully extended and body erect. (12 seconds.)

Syracuse University. When he arrived, Syracuse had won only six of its last 47 games. In just one year he reversed the fortunes and won eight of 21 starts, his only losing effort. A year later, the Orange earned an NIT berth with a 17–8 record. Dave Bing, NBA Rookie of the Year in 1966–67, sparked the Orange to the NCAA Eastern Regional finals in 1966 and a 22–6 record. In 1968 Dr. Lewis became chairman of the athletic department at Sacramento State College.

⑦ LEG EXTENSION—22 seconds
(Hamstring-Calf-Buttocks)
(10 second isometric contraction 12 seconds each leg)

Anchor unit 18 inches above floor. Remove handles and attach web loop with slide to either end of line. Lie on back with head toward unit. Place one leg in upright position, as illustrated, other leg in extended position (parallel to floor.) Keep toes pointed, legs extended and knees locked. Bring one leg upward and over body as far as possible. With pressure on trail line from opposite leg, hold 10 second isometric contraction. Without relaxing, move straightened leg in a straight downward sweep, keeping knee locked through range of motion. Resistance is set by the amount of pressure applied by other leg which controls how fast the exercise can be completed. While maintaining resistance, opposite leg moves upward to exercise position and exercised leg assumes control of resistance to repeat.

⑥ ROWING—22 seconds

Use rowing handle.

Anchor unit 18 inches above floor. Sit with feet against wall, knees bent in Rowing position. Pull with maximum effort for the 10 second isometric contraction (this exercise places less stress on lower back than the Big Four). Without relaxing, pull through with a complete rowing motion until legs are straight on floor and you are lying on your back (4 seconds). Without relaxing, continue to pull handle to chin. (Clean - 4 seconds) and then press until arms are completely extended over head. (Press - 4 seconds.)

⑧ LEG DRIVE—22 seconds (Quadricep) (10 second isometric contraction 12 seconds each leg.)

Anchor unit 18 inches above floor. Remove handles and attach web loop with slide to either end of line. Lie on back with head toward unit. Do not point toes. Fully extend one leg (parallel to floor) controlling trail line. Bring the other thigh as close to the body as possible and bend knee. Drive the bent leg against the resistance, isolating and working the quadricep muscles. Without relaxing, press bent leg straight out, maintaining maximum resistance through range of motion. While maintaining resistance, opposite leg moves into bent position and opposite leg assumes control of resistance to repeat exercise.

⑨ SIT UP—22 seconds

Anchor unit 6 inches above floor, using rowing handle. Bend knees, keeping feet flat on floor. Hold handle at base of neck with overhand grip, as illustrated. Hold 10 second isometric contraction with body at 45 degree angle, shoulders off floor. Without relaxing, release trail line and move forward until elbows touch knees (12 seconds.)

© 1968 Exer-Genie, Inc. EXER-GENIE is a registered trademark of Exer-Genie, Inc.

120

INDIVIDUAL SUPPLEMENTAL DRILLS

BASEBALL PASS

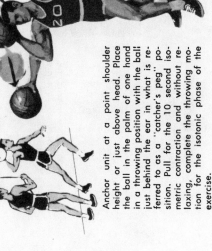

Anchor unit at a point shoulder height or just above head. Place the ball in the palm of one hand in a throwing position with the ball just behind the ear in what is referred to as a "catcher's peg" position. Pull for the 10 second isometric contraction and without relaxing, complete the throwing motion for the isotonic phase of the exercise.

⑩ JUMPING DRILL— 22 seconds

Remove handle, attach harness to end of line. Stand on footboard, or floorplate, feet apart, assume semi-crouch position. Place harness on shoulders, (see accessories) as illustrated, with line down front of body, controlling resistance with trail line in hand. Exert maximum resistance and hold for 10 second isometric contraction, pushing upward. Without relaxing, using maximum resistance, straighten legs and complete exercise wth toe raise (12 seconds).

NOTE: If harness accessory is not available repeat BIG FOUR exercise.

(BALL HANDLING—Use basketball with teather hook or attach S' hook with several wraps of ³/₄'' reinforced filament tape to basketball and hook to end of line.)

TWO HAND OVERHEAD PASS

Anchor unit overhead. Grasp the ball with both hands directly above and slightly behind the head. Exert maximum pull comparable to the tricep exercise for 10 seconds. Then, without relaxing, complete the motion of the two hand overhead pass, bringing the ball directly over the head to a follow-through position in front of the body and still above the head.

ONE HAND SHOVEL PASS OR BOWLING PASS

Anchor unit 18'' above floor. Follow same fundamental procedures as in Two Hand Overhead Pass.

REBOUNDING—
(Coach control)

Anchor to high overhead fixture. Set resistance low and use coach control. Attach long line to rebound basketball. As coach controls height, motion and resistance of ball, player jumps, pulls ball down and moves out. Constant variation does not permit relaxation of players in controlling rebounds. Simulates game conditions.

© 1968 Exer-Genie, Inc. EXER-GENIE is a registered trademark of Exer-Genie, Inc.

122

EXER-GENIE® EXERCISER

Efficiency in Exercise

THE EXER-GENIE® EXERCISER CIRCUIT

- Always begin each exercise period with easy bending and stretching.
- A workout should take from 10 to 30 minutes.
- One repetition is recommended in the circuit exercises.
- As strength increases, the intensity of the workout should also increase.
- The exercise period precedes each basketball practice session and game and should be continued throughout the season.
- Supplemental exercises are recommended for additional training.
- Resistance of the exerciser will be determined by the amount of pressure applied to the trail line by the person not actively involved in the exercise.

NOTE: Using the EXER-GENIE exerciser in the 'buddy system', resistance can be set at 10 pounds for high school—20 pounds for college and professional.

① BIG FOUR—22 seconds

1. Anchor unit to footboard - use rowing handle.
2. Assume deadlift position. Hold isometric contraction for ten seconds, working all major muscle groups.
3. Lift with legs and back, arms straight, rotating hips forward to standing position—(4 seconds.)
4. Arms in clean position, raise handle to chin—(4 seconds.)
5. Rotate hands, palms outward, complete military press—(4 seconds.)

② LATS PULLEY—22 seconds

1. Anchor unit to wall above head level for tallest member of squad, use rowing handle.
2. Grasp handle with arms extended, elbows locked, contract isometrically by pulling down for ten seconds.
3. Without relaxing, release trail line, move handle down across front of body to waist position, keeping arms fully extended, body erect.

TEN STATION CIRCUIT DESIGNED FOR BASKETB

By DR. FRED LEWIS

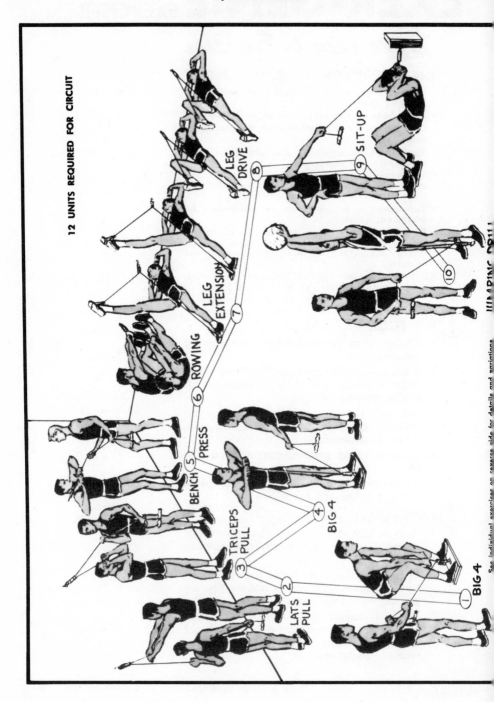

NOTE: It is recommended that the line be shortened in this exercise so that the line will be pulled all the way through at the completion of the exercise and there will be no need to pull the line back to repeat the exercise.

③ TWO ARM TRICEP PULL—22 seconds

1. Anchor unit to wall above head level of tallest member of squad, use rowing handle.
2. Stand with back to wall, grasp handle, hold at top of head, elbows in tight.
3. Exert maximum isometric contraction for ten seconds.
4. Release trail line. Keeping elbows at 45 degree angle, move immediately through range of motion, until elbows at sides.
5. From this position extend arms out straight and then down to waist position.

④ REPEAT BIG FOUR—22 seconds

⑤ BENCH PRESS—22 seconds

1. Anchor unit to wall just above shoulder height of shortest person on squad. Other team members must bend knees to properly position unit above shoulder.
2. Grasp handle, elbows in bench press position, hold ten second isometric contraction pushing to maximum against handle.
3. Release trail line, without relaxing, push handle forward, extending arms away from body.

NOTE: It is recommended that a 24 inch bar be used in this exercise in place of rowing handle to afford a wider hand set.

⑥ ROWING EXERCISE—22 seconds

1. Anchor unit 18 inches above floor.
2. Sit with feet against wall, knees bent in rowing position, hold ten second isometric contraction.
3. Pull through with a complete rowing motion until legs are straight on floor and you are lying on back.
4. Without relaxing, continue to pull handle to chin (Clean) and then press until arms are completely extended over head (press.)

NOTE: This exercise places less stress on lower back than the Big Four.

⑦ LEG EXTENSION (Hamstring-Calf-Buttocks)—22 seconds
(10 sec. isometric - 12 sec. each leg)

1. Anchor unit 18 inches above floor. Remove handles and attach web loops with slide.
2. Lie on back, head toward unit. Place one leg in upright position other leg in extended position (parallel to floor.) Keep toes pointed, legs extended and knees locked.
3. Bring one leg upward and over body as far as possible. With pressure on trail line from opposite leg, do ten second isometric and then move with a straight downward sweep, keeping knee locked through range of motion.
4. While maintaining resistance, opposite leg moves upward to exercise position and exercised leg assumes control of resistance to repeat exercise.

NOTE: Two units are required for this exercise.

⑧ LEG DRIVE—22 seconds

1. Anchor unit 18 inches above floor. Remove handles and attach web loops with slide.

2. Lie on back, head toward unit.

3. Do not point toes. Bring one thigh as close to body as possible and bend knee. Opposite leg is extended. controlling trail line.

4. After ten second isometric contraction, press bent leg straight out, maintaining maximum resistance through range of motion.

5. While maintaining resistance, opposite leg moves into bent position and opposing leg assumes control of resistance to repeat exercise.

NOTE: Two units are required for this exercise.

⑨ SIT UP—22 seconds

1. Anchor unit 6 inches above floor, use rowing handle.

2. Bend knees, keep feet flat on floor.

3. Hold handle at base of neck with overhand grip. Hold ten second isometric contraction with body at 45 degree angle, shoulders off floor.

4. Release trail line and without relaxing, move forward until elbows touch knees.

⑩ JUMPING DRILL—22 seconds

1. Attach unit to floorplate. Use shoulder harness in place of handle.

2. Place feet in jumping position a bit wider than shoulder width, preferably staggered. Place harness on shoulders (see accessories) with line in front of body.

3. Assume semi-crouch position and with ball in hands, exert maximum 10-second contraction, pulling upward.

4. Without relaxing, while raising ball overhead, continue to straighten legs finishing with a toe raise.

NOTE: It is preferable to place a basketball in hands to maintain balance. This can only be done when using the buddy system in this drill.

RUNNING DRILLS: (Recommended for use at the end of each practice session)

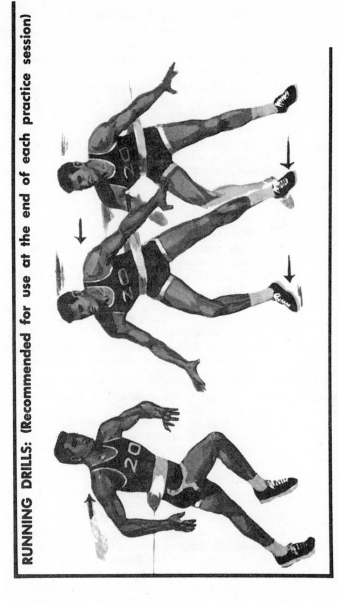

© 1968 Exer-Genie, Inc. EXER-GENIE is a registered trademark of Exer-Genie, Inc.

harness at each end (see accessories). Anchor unit near floor level. (One unit is recommended for each two members of the team.) In using the 'buddy system' place each harness around mid section of participants and join ends of harness with 'S' hook. Place towel beneath 'S' hook at mid section to avoid irritation.

One player runs forward to end of line while partner in harness walks back to point of anchor. Returning player then runs forward, alternating three trips forward, three trips backward, three trips to the side going to the left and three trips to the right. Maintain a 30 second count for each trip. If player reaches end of line before the 30 seconds he should run in place. Proper form and running technique can be easily corrected in this drill.

TIP DRILL

Bill Mulligan

Riverside City College

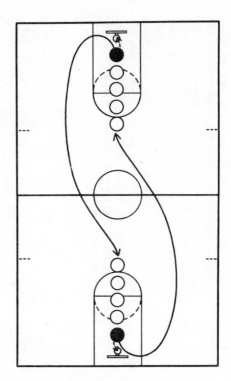

On the whistle, tipping against the board begins at both ends of the court. After tipping the ball on the board, the player must go to the other end to tip the ball on that board. If either ball hits the floor, the drill is begun again. The players must go three minutes without allowing the ball to touch the floor before the drill ends.

Special Value of the Drill

The drill is a *tremendous* conditioner. The players hate it but the coaches love it! It is run at the end of practice only.

When Bill Mulligan took over as head coach at Riverside City College in 1966, he had to follow one of the greatest of success stories—that of Jerry Tarkanian, who had achieved about all there is to achieve in junior college basketball. But Bill Mulligan had a pretty distinguished record in his own right. Overall, he had a lifetime record of 233–41. Since coming to Riverside he has compiled a record of 61 wins against 26 losses.

CONDITIONING DRILL WITH FUNDAMENTALS

Harlan Murdoch
Gordon College

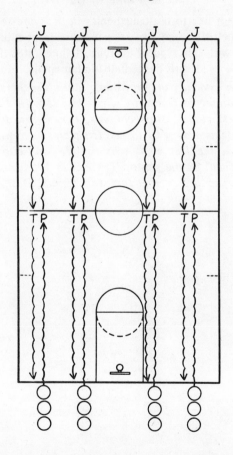

The squad is divided into even-numbered groups. The players stand in line formation on the baseline. The first man from each group has the basketball, and when the whistle blows they dribble with their right hand to the center line. Upon reaching this part of the court they stop their dribble and do five quick push-ups. When they complete this, they pick up the ball and dribble with their left hand to the end of the court. Holding the ball under their arm, they jump five times, reaching up with their

right hand to tap the wall. They then dribble with either hand back to the center line where they stop again and, standing straight-legged, touch the floor five times with both hands. Then they pick up the ball, dribble to their respective lines, and give the ball to the next man in the group. Each group continues until they finish the dribbling calisthenics drill. This may be used as a competitive drill. This type of conditioning along with fundamentals can be used with passing and shooting fundamentals also. The young men certainly enjoy this variation that is included in their pre-season training.

Special Value of the Drill

For those who still like to use calisthenics in their pre-season training sessions, this drill helps to take away the old stigma of monotony which was once associated with this type of exercise. It integrates the certain type of calisthenics to be used with basketball fundamentals.

Harlan Murdoch coached at Aroostook State Teachers College for one season before coming to Gordon College in 1956. In 13 seasons at Gordon College in Wenham, Massachusetts, Coach Murdoch has compiled a record of 199 wins against 97 losses. His teams have won five conference championships in the last eight seasons. He was chosen small college "Coach of the Year" by the Boston Traveler *in 1964, and in 1967 he was given the same honor by the James Naismith Basketball Conference coaches.*

7

Two- and Three-Man Offensive Drills

The number of methods and patterns that have been devised to set up scoring opportunities for the players is enormous. Practice drills must, of course, be built around the offensive system selected by the coach, but, in all probability, will contain the basic elements of offensive play: passing, screening, dribbling, cutting, pivoting, shooting, and rebounding. By utilizing the part method of teaching and by giving careful attention to these fundamental skills within the basic framework of the style of attack, the coach is able to establish a sound system of offensive play.

THREE-ON-THREE CONTINUITY

Don Donoher

University of Dayton

The ball begins with the coach. He passes to O3 and O1 makes a cut off O2's screen, either baseline or over the top. O2 holds the screen and then drifts out to replace O1. O3 looks for O1 inside or goes one-on-one with his man, X3. If O3 does neither, he passes back to the coach, who reverses the ball to O2. Now O3 off O1's screen and the continuity is now on.

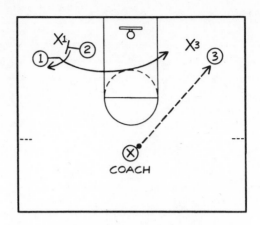

Special Value of the Drill

(Offense)—Each player experiences a turn in the post as a screener or shooter, as an outside man with the ball either passing or going one-on-one, and as a cutter (Shuffle or California) without the ball.

(Defense)—It gives the players work at defending an outside man with the ball and without the ball, a weakside man going off a screen, and an inside man flashing to the post. The defensive men can or cannot switch, depending on the coach's rules for the drill. Rebounding is also a big part of this drill.

Don Donoher came to the University of Dayton in 1964 as an assistant to Coach Tom Blackburn. Before this he had served as a scout for Coach Blackburn for eight years. In 1964, Donoher was awarded the head coaching job. The 1966–67 Flyers competed in their third consecutive NCAA Tournament, advancing to the finals against UCLA before losing. In 1967–68 their 17–9 season record earned them an invitation to the NIT and, led by MVP Don May, the Flyers disposed of West Virginia, Fordham, Notre Dame, and Kansas to win and finish the season 21–9. The 1968–69 team was also a 20-game winner, bringing Coach Donoher's career record to 111–35.

OFFENSIVE BACKDOOR DRILL

Frank Ellis

West Virginia Wesleyan College

The offensive man with the ball is being over-played by the defensive man so as to prevent the offensive man from passing the ball to his teammate and going behind him for a set shot. Only one defensive man

134

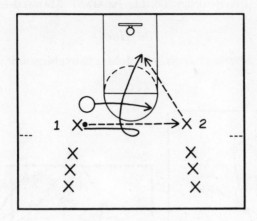

is used for the drill. He is told to over-play the man who has the ball and prevent him from going behind the man to whom he passed the ball. As soon as the man with the ball who starts the drill sees that he is over-played, he yells "check" to let his teammate know of his immediate future maneuver. After passing the ball, he runs toward his teammate, stops with left foot extended toward his teammate who now has the ball, extends his left arm up and makes a fist and yells "check" again, then does a reverse pivot with his right foot as the pivot foot, and cuts for the basket. He can expect an over-the-head pass or a bounce pass from his teammate. The defensive man has the option of leaving his original man and trying to bottle up the man with the ball or recovering after his over-play and covering his original man who is breaking for the basket. Number 2 man must be able to deliver the ball to the cutter with an over-the-top pass or take a dribble and deliver a bounce pass to the cutter. If the defensive man sags back and guards the cutter, the Number 2 man will dribble to the foul line for a jump shot.

Special Value of the Drill

The drill is designed to teach the offensive player not to throw the ball too soon to a teammate who is being overplayed and thus giving the defense the ball for a possible winning basket. This is just one of the many give-and-go maneuvers that are stressed when playing against the man-to-man defense. I like the drill because you are teaching players to take advantage of the defensive mistake to get an easy two points.

In 19 years of coaching at West Virginia Wesleyan College, Frank Ellis has compiled a record of 283 wins against 227 losses. His teams have twice been quarter finalists in the NAIA Tournament (1957–58 and 1959–60). His 1958–59 team had a record of 34–2, and he was named 1959 West Virginia College Coach of the Year. He is presently a member of the Olympic Basketball Committee for the United States.

OUT OF BOUNDS DRILL AGAINST MAN-TO-MAN

Jim Hart

Matthews High School, Matthews, Missouri

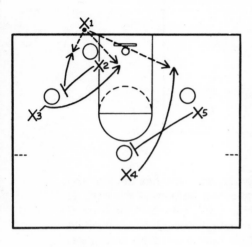 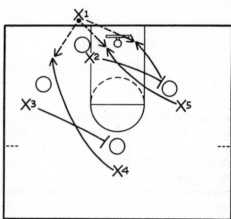

On the slap of the ball, X2 breaks to either X3 or X5 and sets a screen. If he goes to X3, X5 sets a screen for X4 and stays out on defense. As X2 screens X3, X3 breaks to the basket. If a switch does not occur, X3 will be wide open. If there is a switch, X2 has O3 on a roll back to the basket or to the baseline. In the option X2 screens for X5 with X3 screening X4.

Special Value of the Drill

This is a good drill to teach men to get free when the ball is out of bounds under the bucket. As long as a team is in a man-to-man defense, it is impossible to stop this maneuver.

Jim Hart began his coaching career at East Prairie, Missouri, in 1963. In 1966 he became the basketball coach at Matthews High School in Matthews, Missouri. During three seasons he has recorded 92 wins against only seven losses. This includes three undefeated conference seasons and conference tournaments. His team won the Class M Missouri State title in 1968 and lost in the quarter-final game of the state in 1969. His team was picked No. 1 team in Southeast Missouri in 1967 and 1968, and No. 2 team in 1969. He was voted the Coach of the Year Award in Southeast Missouri in 1968.

One-on-One Drill

Paul D. Hinkle

Butler University

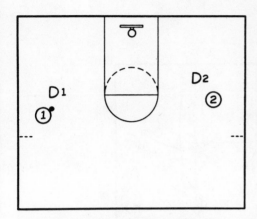 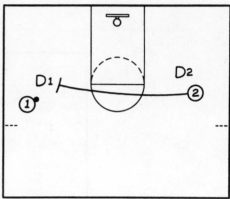

O1 has the ball and fakes and dribbles, shoots from the outside, or drives to the basket against D1. O2 is the follow-in man. D2 must prevent O2 from getting missed shot. In Diagram 2, O2 sets screen for O2 and cuts away for return pass or follows the shot. O1 dribbles by the screen for the shot or return passes to O2.

Special Value of the Drill

This drill involves the basics of basketball. Offensively, it requires individual cleverness and gives practice in a two-man screen offense. Defensively, it places responsibility on the individual and teaches the player to handle defensive situations on screens.

Tony Hinkle, the acknowledged dean of Indiana coaches and regarded as the foremost three-sport mentor in the country, has completed his 40th year as Butler basketball coach. He came to Butler in 1921 as assistant to the late Pat Page, helped tutor the Bulldogs to a national basketball championship in 1924, then took the reins on his own in 1926 and came up with a second national title for Butler in 1929. He owns a career total of 617 basketball triumphs—546 at Butler, 71 at Great Lakes; he is a member of both the James Naismith Memorial Basketball Hall of Fame and the Helms Foundation Hall of Fame. Butler's fieldhouse is now Hinkle Fieldhouse in tribute to his 48 years of dedicated service to Butler. Coach Hinkle is a former president of the National Collegiate Basketball Coaches Association and 1962 winner of that group's top award for his contributions to the betterment of the game; he also has been instrumental in the development of the basketball rules as a long-time member of the NCAA rules committee.

Post Cut Drill

Gerald Jones

Phoenix Union High School, Phoenix, Arizona

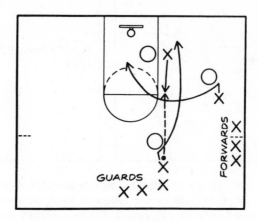

After the guard passes to the center, the first option is the forward back-door; if the forward doesn't break, the guard and the forward split the post with the man feeding the post going first. The players are alert to the possibility of a pick and roll. The players also work the split by passing to the forward, having the forward feed the post and breaking first.

Special Value of the Drill

The drill teaches players to feed the post properly, cut off the post, watch for a backdoor opportunity, and effectively use the pick and roll.

Gerald Jones began his coaching career at Duncan High School in Arizona where, during five years of service, he won 79 while losing 42. From Duncan High he moved to Coolidge High School and recorded 143 wins against 71 losses over a nine-year period. In 1959 he became the basketball coach at Phoenix Union High School in Phoenix, Arizona. In ten seasons he has compiled 178 wins against 53 losses while winning five Christmas Tournaments, six divisional titles, and four state titles. In a career that spans 24 years of coaching, his record stands at an amazing 400 wins against 166 losses.

THREE-ON-TWO COMPETITIVE DRILL

Abe Lemons

Oklahoma City University

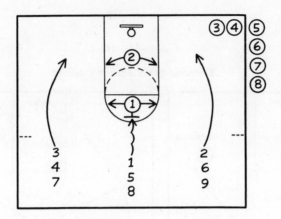

This is a half court drill. Five minutes are put on the clock. 1, 2, and 3 run a three-on-two break and they must score on the first shot to get two points. If they miss, the defense gets two points. If an offensive man rebounds, he gets one more shot (without a pass). If he scores he gets one point for the offense. The offense is allowed one pass inside the free throw circle or free throw line extended (they can pass back out—a total of two passes). If the offense chooses not to shoot, they can throw the ball back out and all they lose is time. They are not allowed to throw out without shooting twice in a row. This drill can be run two-on-one also. After five minutes the other team goes on offense and the first team goes on defense, keeping the same score. The high score wins the ten-minute drill. It can, of course be run for more or less time. A foul results in two points for the offense.

Special Value of the Drill

The drill teaches good speed shooting. It gives the offense and the defense responsibility which shows on the clock. It keeps a large group busy and is popular with the players.

The 1968–69 basketball season marked the 22nd year of involvement with Oklahoma City University athletics for Abe Lemons. During 14 years as head coach of the Chiefs, Lemons compiled an enviable record of 246 wins and 134 losses. He has also tutored six All-America selections, and his teams have participated in eight post-seasons tournaments. The Chiefs have captured the All-College Tournament Crown three times and been runner-up on six occasions during Coach Lemon's tenure. Coach Lemons is not only one of the most successful coaches in basketball, he is also one of the most sought-after lecturers and banquet speakers in the country. His quick wit and refreshing coaching outlook prompted Sports Illustrated *to state that "the funniest man in basketball is Abe Lemons."*

SIX-MAN DRILL

Gary Marriott

Trinidad State Junior College

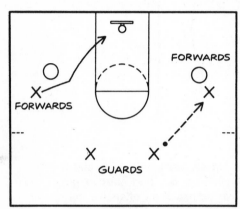 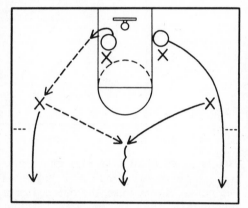

After making the G to F pass the forwards go two-on-two. Every time the ball is strong side, the weak-side forward pinches in on the free throw line. If the strong-side forward cannot drive, the weak-side forward comes up on a backdoor. After shot is taken, all four forwards crash the boards. As soon as the defensive forward gets the rebound he passes the ball out to the guard in the outlet zone. After the outlet pass is made, the ball is passed back to the middle to the other guard and a forward fills the other lane in a three-man fast break.

Special Value of the Drill

An excellent drill for coordinating an offensive attack with defensive assignments and a fast break.

Gary Marriott began his coaching career in 1964 when he became the basketball coach at Boswell Junior High School in Topeka, Kansas. His team was 11–0, winning the City Championship. The next year he moved to Manhattan High School in Manhattan, Kansas, where he remained for two seasons. His record during those two years was 44–8 and included a league championship and an appearance in the state tournament. In 1967 he became the basketball coach at Armstrong High School in Armstrong, Iowa. After one season there, he accepted the head basketball post at Trinidad Junior College in Trinidad, Colorado.

SCREEN AND ROLL DRILL

Frank McGuire
University of South Carolina

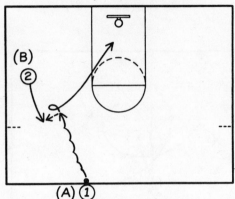

Form two lines: one back court (A); one in the corner (B). #1 dribbles toward #2 who comes from the corner. #1 stops and passes off to #2. #1 sets post, then rolls toward basket, looking over his shoulder for a return pass from #2.

#2, who comes from the corner and gets the ball from #1, has the option of shooting over the set-screen or passing to #1 if there is a pick-off.

The drill is practiced on both sides of both half-court areas.

Special Value of the Drill

The drill is very effective because ball-handling, dribbling, shooting, and passing-off are all involved.

Frank McGuire is one of only three coaches in the history of college basketball to be twice-named as national Coach-of-the-Year. He is the only coach to receive this honor at two different schools, the only man to take teams from different schools to the NCAA basketball finals, and the only man to take teams in two different sports, basketball and baseball, to NCAA championships. McGuire-coached basketball squads have participated in four NCAA and four NIT tournaments. His 1957 North Carolina team won the National title with a 32–0 record. He began his long and brilliant coaching career at Xavier High School, where he compiled a 126–39 record over an 11-year period. His overall record at St. John's was 103–35 for five seasons. In 1953 he accepted an offer to go to the University of North Carolina. His records there from 1956–61 ran 18–5, 32–0, 19–7, 20–5, 18–6, and 19–4. His teams captured four regular-season championships. After the 1960–61 season, he became the coach of the Philadelphia Warriors of the NBA. When Philadelphia shifted their franchise to San Francisco, McGuire spent a year in public relations work and came to the University of South Carolina in the spring of 1964.

TRIPLE SPLITTING THE POST

Bob Polk

St. Louis University

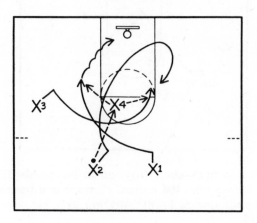

X4 assumes the high post with X1 and X2 as the guards. X3 will set up at a forward position at the foul line extended. Anyone may pass to X4 with X2 faking to the right and making the first cut, X3 the second cut, and X1 the last cut. Any one of the cutters may be given the ball.

Special Value of the Drill

The drill is excellent for developing and establishing movement, faking and footwork to get free, ball handling, and the timing necessary for coordiated team play. It is also a good conditioner.

Bob Polk, who was voted the 1968 NCAA College Division Coach of the Year, has been the architect of basketball powerhouses at both Vanderbilt University and Trinity University. He built Vanderbilt into a perennial challenger for the Southeastern Conference crown from 1947–61 and he transformed Trinity into a giant-killer from 1965–69. In 1969 he became the 16th coach in the history of St. Louis University basketball after compiling an outstanding 266–134 record in 18 years at Vanderbilt and Trinity. Polk's Vandy teams posted a record of 197–106 during 14 seasons. In 1965 he was appointed head basketball coach at Trinity and, in four seasons, he compiled a 69–28 record. In 1967–68 Trinity placed third in the NCAA Small College Tournament with a 23–8 record, and Coach Polk was named by the National Association of Basketball Coaches, of which he is a director, as the 1968 NCAA College Division Coach of the Year.

Three-Man Cut Drill

Al Shaw

Williams College

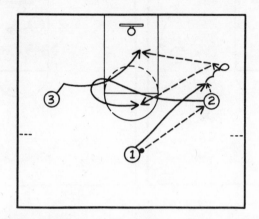

1 passes to 2 and follows his pass, going inside the defensive man for a return pass. He dribbles and uses a reverse pivot to pass to 3 as the first option or 2 as the second option. As 2 cuts after the hand-off *he watches the ball* **and keeps his left hand up as if to receive the pass on his cut.**

Special Value of the Drill

It is a good screening drill. It may also be used for the layup or for the jump shot at the top of the key.

Al Shaw has completed 20 years as coach of the Williams College Basketball team. Since Shaw took over in 1949, the Ephs have won 253 games, and lost 135 for an average of .654. With student athletes (there are no athletic scholarships at Williams), Coach Shaw has put three teams into the NCAA Tourney—the teams of 1955, 1959, and 1961. His 1961 team was eliminated by Wittenburg, the eventual winner. In Little Three competition, Williams College, under Shaw's leadership, has won nine titles and shared five. Through the years Shaw's teams have won eight and lost ten against Ivy League representatives Dartmouth, Harvard, and Columbia.

Driving Offensive Man Drilling to Kick Ball Out to Teammate Against Sagging Defense

Paul Valenti

Oregon State University

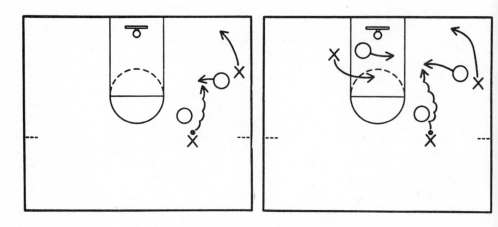

Instruct sagging man to vary the toughness of his sag. Sometimes he will come hard and other times he will fake a move at the offensive man. The offensive man must then play the situation properly, either by driving all the way to the basket or kicking the ball out when he is really challenged. Defensive man should give the ball handler the advantage of at least a step so that he can make the drive. The drill could also be set up to include the postman and his defensive man, or for any outside offensive position.

Special Value of the Drill

The drill is especially valuable because it sets up a very true defensive and offensive situation encountered by all offensive players.

In four seasons as Oregon State University Head Basketball Coach, Paul Valenti has won a Pacific Conference championship, finished second once, and fourth once. In 1966–67 nobody gave Oregon State University even a remote chance to win the PAC-8 crown, but Coach Valenti and his Beavers surprised all and reached the finals of the Western Regional NCAA Tournament. In that year he was named "West Coast Coach of the Year." In 1965 Valenti replaced the late Slats Gill on his retirement from coaching. He had loyally served as Slats Gill's top assistant for 18 years and was well prepared for his new post. In four seasons Valenti has a lofty 63–44 win and loss record.

8

Defensive Drills

As offensive play improves, the role of defense gets tougher. More time is required in practice today to teach the players to handle the complexities of defensive play against a very wide variety of offensive styles of play. Physically, good defense requires excellent balance, correct use of the feet and hands, vision on-and-off the ball, and proper body position. Mentally, it requires aggressiveness, determination, intelligence, and initiative. Both areas are important in developing a sound system of defense, and each must receive a great deal of attention daily in the practice session.

DEFENSIVE PRESSURE DRILL

Stan Albeck

University of Denver

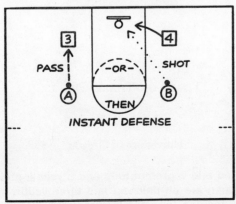

The drill starts with the defensive man (A) passing to the guard (3) and then attempting to stop him from bringing the ball up court. If the offensive man can bring the ball to mid court, he gets a point. They then change positions and the same drill is started over at the mid court line. The first player to score ten points is the winner. Another method of conducting the drill is to have B attempt a field goal with 4 rebounding the ball and bringing it up while the defense plays tough and aggressive. The scoring method is the same in this game, with the winners meeting to determine a champion.

Special Value of the Drill

The drill has merit other than the obvious conditioning involved. It develops the footwork ability of the defensive player with the sudden reactions to changes by the offensive man, and it is useful as an exercise in constantly checking the position of the defense. Players are instructed to gamble for the interceptions and steals, anticipating the offensive moves. While the defensive ability is of major magnitude in this drill, it is also an asset to the ball handlers in facing the opponent's press.

Stan Albeck brought a 194–82 collegiate coaching record to the University of Denver. He had previously served as head coach at Adrian (Michigan) College and at Northern Michigan University the past 12 years. He was named head basketball coach at Adrian College in Michigan in June, 1956, where his Bulldog team posted a 16–5 record and won the NAIA District 23 Championship. The following season he moved to Northern Michigan University in Marquette, Michigan, and in 11 years became the Wildcats' most successful coach, winning 178 and losing 77 against top-flight competition. His Northern Michigan squads won five Michigan NAIA titles. His 1960–61 squad placed third in the NAIA Finals in Kansas City and his 1962–63 team reached the quarter finals.

THREE-ON-THREE DRILL

Steve Belko

University of Oregon

The squad is divided into a green group and a yellow group. Three team members of the green are on defense, and three yellow group members are on offense in position to simulate three-man motion. Not much at-

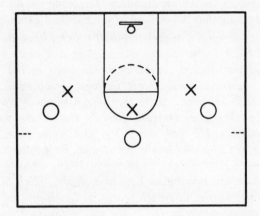

tention is given to matching size although this is preferable later in the year when using a scouting report. The defensive team must stop the yellow team from scoring or they stay on defense. The thing that makes it good is the rigid enforcement of the rules of the drill.

The green team will stay on defense if they: (1) are scored upon; (2) commit a foul; (3) lose a legitimate rebound; (4) make a ridiculous defensive play; (5) permit an uncontested shot inside a designated perimeter area; (6) do not pick up the drive when the opportunity arises; or (7) permit a cutter to receive a pass inside the perimeter area without a legitimate contest.

If the offense does not score, then they will, in turn, go on defense; another green group becomes the offense. The offense has to give up the ball: (1) if they do not score; (2) if they fail to take a good shot in the perimeter area (this is to make them think realistically so that they don't just try to pass the ball and ignore legitimate shots); (3) if there is any violation or foul.

We insist that, when the defensive three do get a rebound, they must look for the outlet pass to set up their break. When they do make it, everybody sprints to the mid court. This gives them the reaction we want off the boards to start break situations. If they forget this, even though they rebound the ball cleanly, we make them stay on defense.

Special Value of the Drill

The secret of this drill, as was previously mentioned, is to enforce the rules and not to feel sorry for the defensive men who stay on defense a number of times. This drill is done early in the year for about 15 minutes a day or longer. Later in the year ten minutes a day is enough.

The players like this drill because it is competitive. There is more opportunity for coaching in this drill than in any of our other drills. We can adapt this three-man drill in a breakdown situation against the opponents we are playing to give us practice against their favorite maneuvers. This also gives everyone an opportunity to play defensive post position, little man against big man, match-up situations, screening out on the boards, and just about everything that is involved in a basketball game.

In 14 seasons as Oregon's head basketball coach, Steve Belko has guided six teams into NCAA tournament competition and twice has led Oregon into the NCAA post-season competition. He came to the Webfoots after six successful seasons at Idaho State College, which included a win and loss record of 108–53, four trips to the NCAA regional playoffs, and four conference titles. While at Oregon, Belko's clubs have won 132 games against 180 setbacks. He took the 1959–60 Oregon team to the NCAA playoffs, losing to California in the semifinals. He began his coaching career at St. Marie's High School in Idaho in 1939, where he remained for a single season before moving to Lewiston, Idaho, High School for three years. He won the district title each season at Lewiston and was runner-up for the state championship in 1941. He joined the staff at the University of Idaho as freshman football and basketball coach in 1946. He remained with the Vandals until the end of the 1950 season, and then accepted the Idaho State position.

GUARDING THE LINE DRILL

Madison Brooks

East Tennessee State University

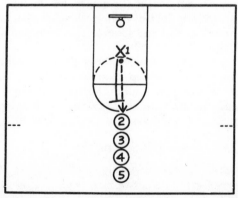

X1 has the ball with his pivot foot on the circle. He makes a direct pass (no bounce) to O2 and then "attacks" him defensively. His main concern is to stop the drive. Other concerns of X1 are to harass shooter, screen out after shot, and go for rebound. If O2 gets rebound he works one-on-one from that position. The drill ends when O2 scores on X1, or X1 gets the rebound. O2 goes to the end of the line. X1 follows this same procedure against O3, O4, O5, etc. until all players in the line have been

guarded. Then O2 goes on defense. The defensive players take one lap for each basket scored against him and one lap for each foul he commits.

Special Value of the Drill

Teaches important fundamentals of defense:

1. Approach to man with ball in scoring territory (body under control looking for drive or fake).
2. Defensing the drive.
3. Defensing the jumper (from top of circle or off drive).
4. Screening out.
5. Rebounding.
6. Aggressiveness.
7. Defensive footwork and body balance.

Madison Brooks came to East Tennessee State University in 1948 after a successful 11-year high school coaching career in which his teams won 165 and lost 54. In 1968 his team won the conference crown and represented the league in the NCAA Mideast Regional playoffs in Kent, Ohio, and Lexington, Kentucky, for the first time in ETSU's history. He also passed another milestone reached by few coaches—on January 29 his Bucs edged Morehead 86–79, to give Coach Brooks his 300th career victory. State's appearance in the NCAA post-season tourney was the school's first. Before that, Brooks-coached Buccaneer teams had represented their district three times in the NAIA Tournaments in Kansas City and once in the NCAA College Division playoffs.

THREE-ON-THREE DRILL

Lee Cabutti

Central High School, Champaign, Illinois

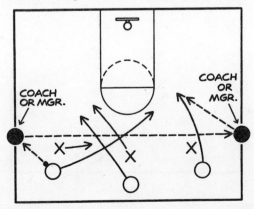

The offense may throw the ball to the coaches and then receive a return pass. They play until the defense gets the ball or the offense scores. The offense can move in any direction it wishes. One coach can throw the ball across court to the other coach.

Special Value of the Drill

This drill teaches the defensive men how to watch the ball and also their man. It is a great peripheral vision drill.

Lee Cabutti began his coaching career in Herrin, Illinois, where, in eight seasons, he compiled a record of 145 wins and 49 losses. In 1957 he moved to Central High School in Champaign, Illinois. In 13 seasons at Central High he has recorded 240 wins against 70 losses. In 1969, Central had a record of 30–4 and finished third in the state. Central has won 78 of its last 90 games. Coach Calbutti's teams have never allowed more than 50 points to their opponents (on a seasonal basis) in his 21 years of coaching.

TWO-MAN DEFENSIVE DRILL

Jim Carey

Ellsworth College

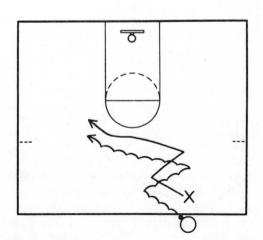

The man with the ball dribbles to one side and then the other while the defensive man forces the dribbler to the inside. The defensive man keeps his hands behind his back. The reason for this is to make him move his feet and not lose position by reaching. This drill is particularly good for the guards. They pick up a man at the mid court line (two-on-two), protecting the middle and beating the man to the outside.

Jim Carey coached four years at Tama, Iowa, where his teams won 72 while losing 14. He became the head basketball coach at Ellsworth College in 1961. His teams won conference titles in 1963–64, 1966–67, and 1967–68, and have been nationally ranked in 1964, 1965, 1966, and 1968. His teams at Ellsworth have had an overall record of 156 wins and 68 losses. In 12 years of coaching he has recorded eight conference championships.

PASS AND POST DEFENSIVE DRILL

Pat Dougherty

San Jose City College

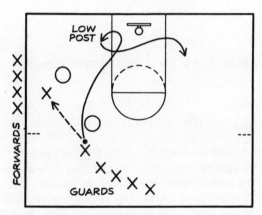

One guard and one forward from each line go on offense and one from each line go on defense. The ball starts with the offensive guard. He must pass to the offensive forward who is attempting to create a lead. The defensive forward does his best to prevent this pass. After the pass is made, the guard makes a quick inside cut to the low post area and doubles back to establish a low post. The defensive guard must stay with the quick cut to prevent the easy layup and then attempt to defense the low post by fronting the post. The offensive forward may not throw the pass over the top. If the forward cannot pass to the low post, the guard will clear out and the forward will go one-on-one with his man. The offensive man then goes to defense and the defensive man goes to the end of the line of offensive players.

Special Value of the Drill

1. The drill teaches the forward to prevent the pass to the offensive forward. Also teaches offensive forward to create a lead.
2. The drill teaches the guard to stay with the guard on the quick inside cut (not to lunge for the ball, leap, trail the man, etc.).
3. It teaches the guard to defense the low post by fronting and preventing a pass. (This seems more and more a part of good offense these days.)
4. It teaches the forward to help with defense on the low post and then make a recovery and go one-on-one on defense.

Pat Dougherty became the head basketball coach at San Jose City College in San Jose, California, in 1966. Formerly head of the Physical Education Department at Blackford High School in San Jose, he compiled a record of 72–12 and led his teams to three consecutive league championships before coming to City College.

RECOVERY FROM LOST BALL SITUATION AGAINST A PRESS

Jim Howard

Central High School, Tulsa, Oklahoma

One of the main things with which a team must contend is the press. Every team works against the press in practice but we try to carry it a step further. The players are taught how to recover quickly after the ball is lost as a result of the press. Not enough work is done by most teams on what to do once the basketball is lost. In practice many coaches stop the action when the ball is lost and chew out the players for making a mistake. Teams get hurt just as much, and probably more, after losing the ball by not being able immediately to adjust mentally to playing defense. One mistake leads to another, and a team can be destroyed mentally in a matter of minutes by the press if they're not prepared to recover quickly after a mistake.

If the ball is lost while combating a pressing team in practice, the team now on defense must beat the team now on the attack to an area designated on the court in order that the other team will not have a numbers advantage. The importance of having all five men reach the area as quickly as possible to play defense is continually stressed, along with an immediate fulfillment of their new offensive assignment once the ball has been recovered. To help create this situation, the coach may blow his whistle; this signals the man with the ball to give it up immediately to the nearest defensive man and simulates a loss of ball situation.

Jim Howard began his coaching career in 1964 at Central High School in Tulsa, Oklahoma. As "B" coach he had teams that recorded 27 wins against 13 losses. He became the head basketball coach in 1966, and since that time has compiled a regular season record of 44 wins against 25 losses. During the 1968–69 season his team was the State AAA Champs. Including competition in their very important summer basketball program, Coach Howard's five-year record now stands at 111 wins and 43 losses.

Defensive Talking Drill

Orrie Jirele

East High School, Green Bay, Wisconsin

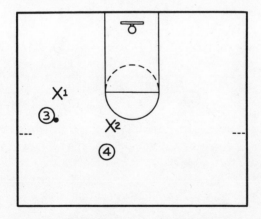

The drill is used mainly for defensive purposes, but it could easily be used for offense as well. Much work is needed on defensive talking. In this drill X2 keeps communicating to X1, "Hep left!"—meaning that X1 has help to his left should the ball be moved in that direction. X1 tries to chase his man to X2 as long as he knows he has help. Should the ball go to O4, then X1 would communicate to X2 that he now has help on his right. X2 can try to chase his man to X1.

Special Value of the Drill

1. Most offensive plays are one-on-one or two-on-two situations and the defensive players must learn how to handle them effectively.
2. It forces the defense to talk and overplay when there are four men on the court.

3. It encourages talking and relaxes the players.
4. It teaches players to know where to expect to find help defensively and how to use that help.

Orrie Jirele began his coaching career in 1965 at Lourdes High School in Rochester, Minnesota, where, during three seasons his teams won 65 games while losing only eight. His teams were State Catholic Champions in 1966, 1967, and 1968. In 1968 he moved to East High School in Green Bay, Wisconsin. In his first season he recorded 17 wins against six losses and a conference championship (first in 17 years), a regional championship, and the sectional runner-up spot.

OVERPLAY AND PRESSURE DRILL

Ross Kershey

Coatesville High School, Coatesville, Pa.

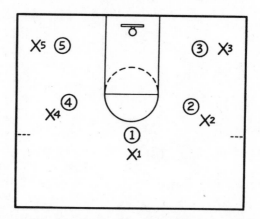

The coach gives the ball to any offensive player and the player dribbles for three seconds. The coach blows the whistle and the dribbler stops wherever he is. His defensive man immediately tightens up, as do all the defensive players. The object is to prevent a successful pass to any offensive player within five seconds. If a successful pass is made to an offensive player, his man gets five laps. If no successful pass can be made, the entire offensive team gets five laps. There is no double-teaming permitted.

Special Value of the Drill

This drill, which emphasizes physical and mental toughness, is an essential for any pressure team. It is a great drill for defensive pressure and overplay, and it also helps the offense get accustomed to pressure and to coming out to meet the ball.

In 13 years at Coatesville High School in Coatesville, Pennsylvania, Ross Kershey has compiled an amazing 255 wins against only 47 losses He began as the J.V. coach, recording 105 wins and 28 losses in a six-year period. In seven years as varsity coach his record is 150 wins and 19 losses. This includes three Ches-Mont League titles and two District One runner-up awards.

Two Drills in One

W. Boyd King

Northeast Missouri State College

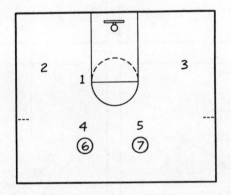

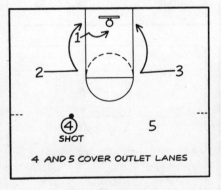

4 AND 5 COVER OUTLET LANES

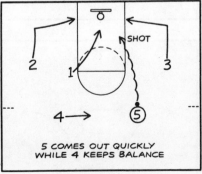

5 COMES OUT QUICKLY
WHILE 4 KEEPS BALANCE

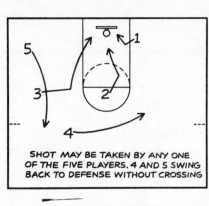

SHOT MAY BE TAKEN BY ANY ONE
OF THE FIVE PLAYERS. 4 AND 5 SWING
BACK TO DEFENSE WITHOUT CROSSING

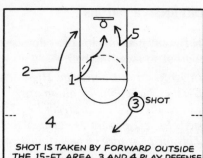

SHOT IS TAKEN BY FORWARD OUTSIDE
THE 15-FT. AREA. 3 AND 4 PLAY DEFENSE
WHILE GUARD (5) GOES TO THE BOARDS

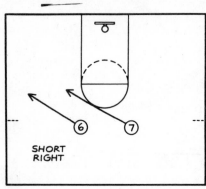

SHORT
RIGHT

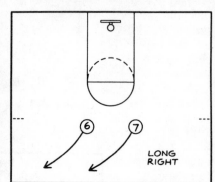

LONG
RIGHT

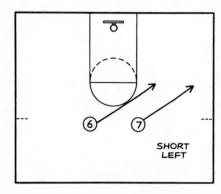

SHORT
LEFT

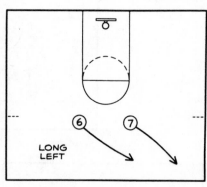

LONG
LEFT

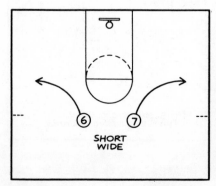

SHORT
WIDE

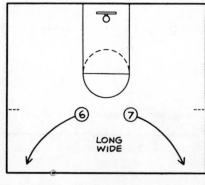

LONG
WIDE

1. Running offensive patterns without a defense. 2. Assuming defensive positions after a shot is taken so as to challenge the outlet pass for the fast break.

While running the offense there are rules as to who rebounds after the shot (see diagrams). Normally in a single pivot the center and forwards rebound unless a forward shoots outside the 15-foot area. If this happens and the forward finds a guard inside him, the forward and guard will exchange duties. This option is not permitted when the guard is very small or very poor on the board. While running offensive patterns without a defense, we try to get our men who are responsible for challenging the outlet pass to immediately assume the correct defensive positions after the offensive shot is taken. These men never cross in getting into position. This means that if a man is caught inside and is not an assigned rebounder, he comes out for defense without changing sides of the court. The other man who is back for defense will move so the inside man will not have to cross court to get into defensive position.

Numbers 1, 2, 3, 4, and 5 run offensive pattern until a shot is taken. Three are assigned to the offensive board (usually 1, 2, and 3) and as soon as the position is assumed, they become teammates of (6) and (7). They then try to get the outlet pass to (6) or (7) in one of the outlet patterns. The men assigned to stop the opponents from starting a break (usually 4 and 5) become defensive men as soon as any member of their team shoots. 4 and 5 must be ready to meet several outlet patterns (see diagrams).

Northeast Missouri State College basketball teams have won 351 games and lost only 177 under Boyd King for a .665 winning percentage. The Bulldogs have been MIAA Champs or Co-Champs six times, finished second eight times, third on five occasions, fourth three times, and sixth once. After a successful high school coaching career, Coach Boyd joined the coaching staff at Northeast Missouri State College in 1946.

TEAM ROTATION DEFENSIVE DRILL

John Manning

Duquesne University

Five offensive men are placed at mid court and are told to run their offense. The defensive team is placed in their usual areas on the court— that is, the big men X5 and X3 on the big men and the other men such as guards X1 and X2 on the outside men. If the defensive team steals the ball twice, everyone rotates. This will eventually allow each man to play under the hoop and the big men will defend the outside men. If a steal is made (an open stance is used on the wing men), the team breaks down court for the score. This threat of a break keeps the offensive team aware of the fast break, thus maintaining proper floor balance. To prevent the defense from over-gambling, a steal can be subtracted whenever the offensive team scores two successive baskets.

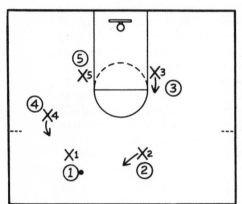 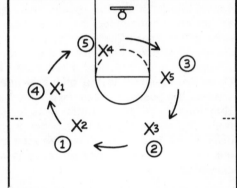

Special Value of the Drill

We are very conscious of team defense at Duquesne. We want all of our players to adapt to all areas on the court. This drill provides us with the necessary practice. It is run early in the season.

John (Red) Manning became Duquesne University's third head basketball coach in 35 years with his appointment in March of 1958. In 1951, he was named coach at Pittsburgh's St. Canice High School where he served for two seasons before returning to Duquesne as an assistant coach under Dudey Moore, a position Manning held for five seasons prior to being named head coach. Taking over the head coaching post during a rebuilding period, he had the Dukes back in national contention in just two seasons. His 1961–62 team finished regular season play with a 20–5 record and received an NIT bid. Losing practically the entire first team from the previous season, he surprised the experts by posting a 13–9 mark during the 1962–63 season. His 1963–64 Dukes chalked up a 16–5 regular season record and received another NIT berth. He reached the coveted "100 Victories" club during the 1964–65 season, his sixth at Duquesne. His 1967–68 team was 18 and 6 and received another NIT bid.

Check Drill

Jack McCloskey

Wake Forest University

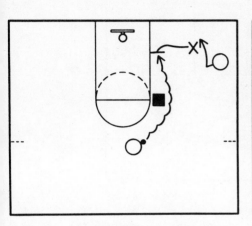 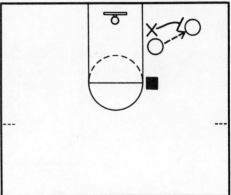

A chair is placed near the foul line and the offensive man starts his drive around the chair (he may not go into the lane). He attempts to make a layup if the defensive man does not play him "square" (nose to nose). The defensive man begins by playing a man in the corner. He has the added responsibility of stopping the drive by forcing an offensive charging foul, or forcing a pass off to the offensive man in the corner. He then must cover his original man and play him in a one-on-one situation.

Special Value of the Drill

The drill develops:

1. *Team* defense.
2. A helping defense.
3. An aggressive and alert defense.
4. A situation that occurs frequently in a game situation.

Jack McCloskey spent ten years at the University of Pennsylvania, his alma mater, before moving south to tackle the job of rebuilding Wake Forest's cage fortunes. He accepted the job in 1966, succeeding Jack Murdock, who has served as acting coach after Horace McKinney resigned in 1965. During his ten years as head coach at Penn his teams won more than 65% of their games his last six years, and only twice in ten seasons did they fall below .500. His record was 146–105, including an 83–53 mark against Ivy League teams. His last team at Penn won the Ivy League Championship.

Two-on-One with a Trailer

John Powless
University of Wisconsin

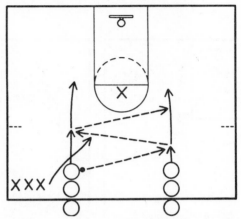

Two offensive men (O) pass back and forth trying to make the defensive man (X) in the middle commit to one side or another. The offensive men will start on the coach's command "Go." The defensive trailer starts on the count of two after the command to go.

Special Value of the Drill

An excellent drill for teaching continuous effort by a defensive trailer against the fast break.

John Powless began his coaching career at the high school level at Tilgham High School, Paducah, Kentucky, in 1957. He then joined the staff at Florida State as an assistant before moving on to Cincinnati in 1960 as freshman basketball coach. His freshman teams at Cincinnati compiled a three-year record of 36–9, including a 15–0 record during the 1962–63 season. He then went to Wisconsin as an assistant coach in 1963, and was appointed head coach of the Badgers in 1968.

Pressure Release Drill

Bud Presley
Santa Ana Junior College

O1 pressures the pass to X1, keeping, whenever possible, vision on both man and ball, making an all-out effort to prevent or deflect the pass. Each time X1 releases and receives the pass he quickly balances up and

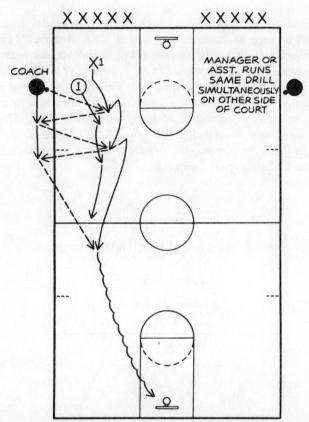

returns the pass to the coach, who follows the action down the court. Any time after at least *three* releases in the back court, X1 breaks fast to the bucket, receives a long pass from the coach, and drives for the layup. O1 recovers as hard as possible and attempts to intercept or contest the layup. X1 and O1 then trade positions and repeat the drill, moving toward the end at which it originated. This drill is run for ten minutes each day during the first month of practice. Note: O1 must not be allowed to play "soft" and anticipate X1's cut to the basket. He must play X1 tight at all times.

Special Value of the Drill

1. It is an excellent progression drill in the man-to-man pressure defense, in which we contest most lead passes.
2. It is extremely valuable in teaching our extended (full and ¾) presses.
3. Offensively, it helps our players learn to "create a lead," i.e., release from pressure and receive a pass.
4. It is an excellent conditioner.
5. It teaches the defensive player to recover as hard as possible to the point of the ball when his man passes him in the press.

*Bud Presley's experience includes 18 years in high school and college
coaching, with an overall basketball record of 283 wins and 117 losses.
While at Cubberley High School in Palo Alto, California, his team set the
SPAL single game (16) and season (36.9) defensive records. In 1960 he
was selected Coach of the Year in the San Francisco peninsula area. In
1965 he became the assistant varsity and head freshman basketball coach
at Gonzaga University in Spokane, Washington. During the 1968–69 season his Gonzaga frosh basketball team won 15 of 18 games, the best in
Zag annals. In 1969 he became the head basketball coach at Santa Ana
Junior College in Santa Ana, California.*

PRESSURE LEAD DRILL

John Rohan

Columbia University

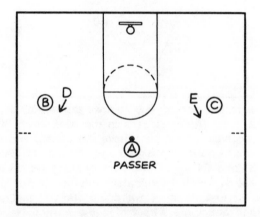

**A is the passer. B and C are on offense and D and E are on defense.
D and E attempt to deny the ball to B and C, thereby giving them work
on defense against a man without the ball. When one of the offensive
men eventually breaks free and receives the ball, the defense immediately must play tough two-on-two defense until they either steal the ball
or rebound it. The men play their positions for three consecutive plays.**

Special Value of the Drill

This drill is extremely simple, yet it encompasses most of the fundamentals
we stress in our pressure man-for-man defense. Before we use this drill
it should be understood that a great deal of time has been spent on one-
on-one defense, over-playing in a one-on-one situation, boxing out, and

recognizing and playing the various two-on-two possibilities. Therefore this drill covers all of these important phases of pressure defense in a highly competitive situation.

John Rohan began his coaching career at Columbia University as the frosh coach, and in 1958 he moved to New York University as the frosh coach. In 1961 he became the head basketball coach at Columbia University. Columbia won the Kodak Classic in 1965, the Steel Bowl in 1966, the Holiday Festival in 1967, and the Ivy League Championship in 1968. In 1968 the New York Metropolitan Basketball Writers Association presented Coach Rohan with the Coach of the Year Award. In major college statistics, his 1967–68 team was sixth in team defense, eighth in win-loss percentages (23–5), sixth in field goal percentage, fourth in average scoring margin, and was ranked sixth in the nation. In his eight seasons at Columbia his record stands at 103–89.

"ROUND-THE-WORLD"

Robert Vaughn

Elizabeth City State College

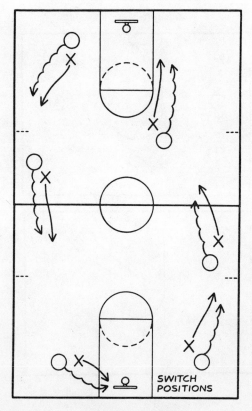

Each offensive man (O) has a ball and must dribble the full court for a short jump shot or layup while the defensive man (X) tries to stop him or contain him without fouling. After the contested shot, the defensive man becomes the offensive man down the other side of the court.

Special Value of the Drill

A very simple but effective drill to teach man-to-man defense and defensive quickness. It also helps the offensive man with his dribbling and ball handling ability. It is an excellent drill for teams who press a lot.

During 19 seasons as head basketball coach at Elizabeth City State College in Elizabeth City, North Carolina, Robert Vaughn has compiled 231 wins against 139 losses. His 1969 Elizabeth City team won the CIAA Championship, the NAIA District 29 Championship, and finished fourth in the NAIA finals in Kansas City.

GUARDING THE MAN AWAY FROM THE BALL

Paul Webb

Randolph-Macon College

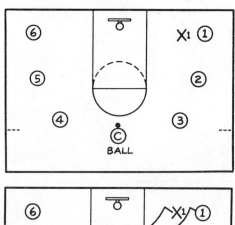

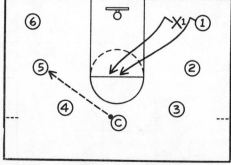

The offensive players form a semi-circle. X1 plays defense on each offensive player around the circle starting with (1). The drill starts with the coach having the ball. X1 assumes a good defensive position on (1). The ball is then passed to one of the offensive players on the opposite side of the floor [(5) in the diagram]. (1) then cuts towards the ball or baseline. If X1 prevents the pass, (1) goes backdoor or (5) shoots. If (1) goes backdoor, X1 defenses the backdoor move. If (5) shoots, X1 blocks out (1) and goes for the rebound. If (1) gets open and receives the pass, X1 plays him one-on-one. The drill ends when X1 gets the ball. X1 then moves to (2) and the drill is repeated. After X1 has been all the way around, we then change defensive men and the drill continues.

Special Value of the Drill

The drill is used primarily as a defensive drill, but we like it because it brings many facets of the game into practice: (1) guarding the man away from the ball; (2) one-on-one if the offensive man receives the pass; (3) rebound block out after the shot; (4) defensing the backdoor play; (5) offensive player getting free to receive the pass; and (6) passer hitting the offensive man as he makes the cut.

In 13 seasons at Randolph-Macon College, Coach Paul Webb has compiled a record of 201 wins against 108 losses. This includes eight state championships, five Mason-Dixon Conference Division Championships, two Mason-Dixon Conference Championships, and two trips to the NCAA Regionals.

FOUR-ON-FOUR

Carroll Williams

Assistant Coach, University of Santa Clara

The squad is broken into four four-man teams. Each team will stay on defense until it has competed against all of the other three teams in succession. End of competition between two teams occurs when offensive scoring or loss of the ball totals five. (One point is awarded to the offense for a basket and one point is given to the defense for a rebound or for a forced turnover. Each team keeps its own score.) At the end of the drill the team who has compiled the greatest number of points is

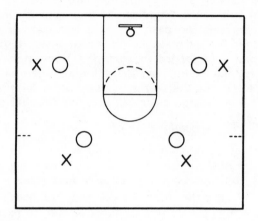

the winning team and usually receives Cokes or some such small reward. Early in the season a great deal of attention is given to defensive
fundamentals of play, and this drill affords the coaches an excellent opportunity to make corrections and teach new techniques during competition. Although it is primarily a defensive drill, special offensive movements are emphasized in an attempt to improve the offensive game.
Many variations may be added. For example, the fast break after a defensive rebound may be included and points given for its successful
execution or for the other team's prevention of it.

Special Value of the Drill

This drill provides one of the best opportunities for teaching defense that
can be devised. It is highly competitive, it teaches court position and the
responsibilities that go along with offensive and defensive play, and it is
an excellent conditioner.

*Carroll Williams started the 1969–70 frosh season with an impressive
102–44 coaching record at the University of Santa Clara. His 1967 team
compiled a 21–1 record and his 1969 team was undefeated at 22–0. The
Santa Clara coach is second on the all-time San Jose State College scoring
list in two categories: single season scoring average (17.0), and total points
in one season (460). He also is a former All-American AAU cager and
was an alternate on the 1960 U.S. Olympic Games team.*

9

Fast Break Drills

All teams will make use of the fast break to some extent during the season, but the coach must decide to what degree he wishes to use it. There are a number of situations from which a fast break can result: short rebound, long rebound, free throw, field goal, jump ball, and interception. Even though a coach does not emphasize the break, it is still a valuable tool for teaching many of the basic skills of basketball when it is presented in the form of a drill. There is no better way to teach and to improve on controlled speed than through fast break drills. They may serve as excellent conditioners, a means of working on passing, and a way in which the combined efforts of the team members can be coordinated.

PROGRESSIVE FAST BREAK DRILL

Alan Balcomb

South Brunswick High School, Monmouth Junction, New Jersey

Diagram 1. The drill usually starts with two-on-one, then goes to three-on-one, and finally three-on-two. In the two-on-one, rapid passing is stressed with no dribbling. This is done in an effort to get the defensive man to stand still as a result of this passing. When the players progress to the three-on-one, passing in the backcourt is stressed.

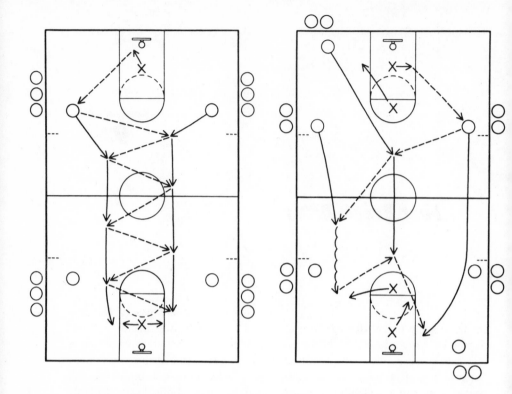

Diagram 2. In the three-on-two situation, the ball is passed in back court and then taken down the side in the front court in order to split the defenders. As soon as the split occurs, the ball is returned to the middle man and he can pass either way or drive up the middle himself. The drill is also run with the rebounder (either offense or defense) staying in the drill as the third man—making the outlet pass and filling the outside lane.

Special Value of the Drill

1. It gives the players practice in game-like break.
2. It gives the players practice in ball handling.
3. The players can practice rebounding and the outlet pass.
4. The players can work on defensing the break.
5. It helps players react to game-like situations.

Alan Balcomb has served as basketball coach at South Brunswick High School in Monmouth Junction, New Jersey, for eight years. During this time he has compiled a record of 97 wins against 75 losses. In 1965 his team played in the Central Jersey semi-finals. In 1966 South Brunswick were Group I finalists and in 1968 they were Central Jersey Group I State Champions.

168

FAST BREAK OUTLET PASS DRILL

Joe Cipriano
University of Nebraska

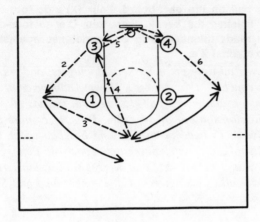

4 throws the ball over the basket for 3 to rebound. 1 wings out for the outlet pass from 3. 2 fills the middle lane by breaking to the top of the key. After 2 gets the ball he stops and passes to 3. 3 puts it on the board for 4 to rebound. 2 breaks to the sideline for the outlet pass and 1 fills the middle. This can be repeated as many times as the coach desires before going on to the four-man fast break.

Special Value of the Drill

1. Teaches players to get proper position on rebounds.
2. Gives the players practice in making the good outlet pass.
3. Teaches the outside players to fill the middle lane properly and make the good pass to the middle man.
4. Keeps a number of men busy working on sound fundamental skills necessary in the fast break.

Joe Cipriano came to Nebraska in 1963 when Cornhusker cage fortunes were at a low ebb. He came to Nebraska from Idaho where his teams posted a rebuilding trail much like Nebraska's: 10–16, 13–13 and 20–6 records. With his six-year record at Nebraska, his win-loss record broke into the winning percentage with 123 victories and 106 defeats. While playing at Washington, he led the Huskies to three straight Pacific Coast division titles and one loop crown. After a short term at high school coaching, he returned to Washington as freshman coach for three seasons before coming to Idaho as the head coach in 1960.

12-MAN FAST BREAK DRILL

Howie Dallmar

Stanford University

The players work in groups of four (X, O, (X)) The coach starts the drill by tossing the ball on the backboard. Four (X)'s go four-on-two against O's. After (X) finishes the break, then four O's go four-on-two against X's. (X)'s then ready themselves to be on defense against X's after O's go four-on-two against X's.

One of Stanford's all-time great basketball players, and today one of the most respected coaches in the country, Howie Dallmar came to Stanford in 1955 and has since compiled a 187–153 record. He has guided the Indians into the first division ten out of 14 years. Prior to coming to Stanford he served for six years as head basketball and baseball coach at the University of Pennsylvania. As head basketball coach at Pennsylvania (1949–54), his teams won 105, lost 51, and were 48–26 against Ivy League opposition. His over-all coaching record at Pennsylvania and Stanford is 302 wins and 204 losses.

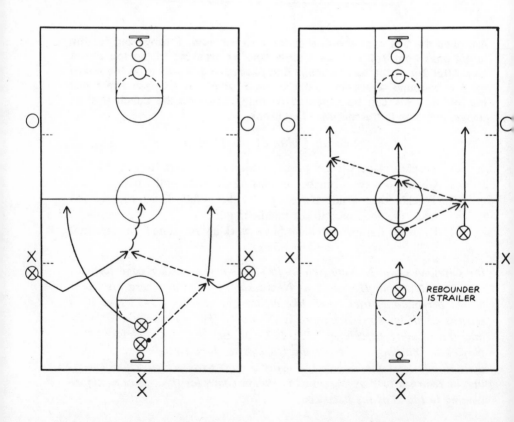

REBOUNDER IS TRAILER

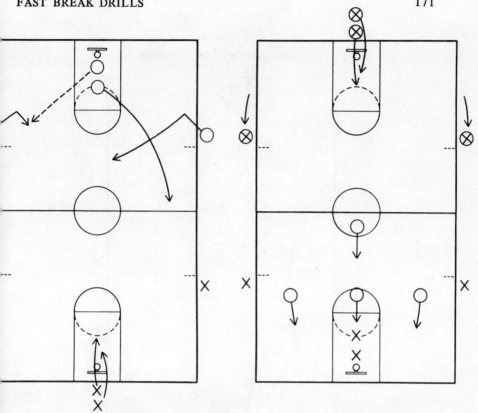

FOUR-MAN MULTIPURPOSE FAST BREAK DRILL

Dick Edwards

University of the Pacific

Forwards and centers form two lines under baskets at both ends of the court. The guards form at the center line on both sides. Two players are defenders at one end. The coach initiates the drill by shooting the ball. After the rebound, the two attacking players make the outlet pass to one of the guards and then fill the lanes. The two defenders defend against the four attackers. They either take the ball out of bounds after a score, or rebound the shot and outlet pass to the next two guards and the attack begins against the two new defenders at the opposite end of the court. The action is continuous until the coach terminates the drill.

Special Value of the Drill

This is a fast-moving, continuous action drill incorporating conditioning, ball handling, and shooting. It teaches players to make a fast transition from defense to offense, to fill the fast break lanes, and to fill the proper spots at the end of the break. It is good practice in defending against the

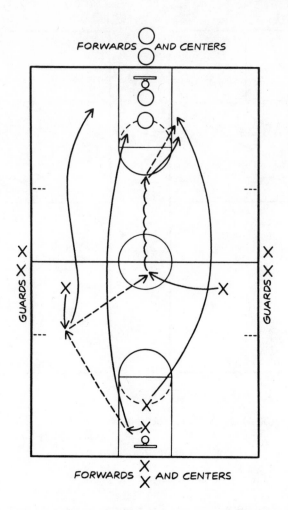

break and it fits well with a pressing defense, teaching the quick strike back after being scored upon. It is an excellent offensive rebounding drill. Players like the drill.

Coach Dick Edwards began his winning ways at Yreka High School in Yreka, California, with a 70–12 mark. He later moved to El Camino High School and posted a 64–9 record in an area where many greats of basketball fame have developed. In his 12 years of coaching, he has won a total of ten tournaments and six conference championships. In his six years at the University of the Pacific his record stands at 110 wins and 51 losses and includes two West Coast Athletic Conference Championships and two trips to the NCAA Regionals. In 1965–66 and 1966–67, he was honored by being chosen "Coach of the Year" in Northern California by the Basketball Writers' Association.

CIRCLE FAST BREAK DRILL

Joe Fields

Lake City Junior College

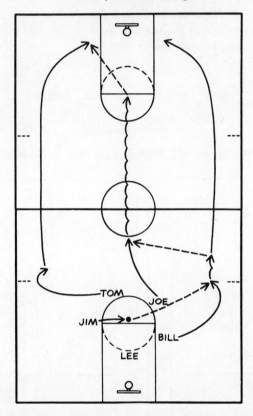

1. Five players are lined up around the circle at the foul line.
2. The coach places the ball on the floor in the middle of the circle.
3. The coach calls out the name of one of the players. For example, he calls Jim's name. Jim jumps into the circle, picks up the ball and throws an outlet pass for the fast break.
4. After receiving the ball, Bill dribbles down the floor and passes to Joe who is the middle man on the break.
5. Bill and Tom fill outside lanes. Jim and Lee are trailers.

Special Value of the Drill

This is a good drill for the fast break. It involves ball handling and filling lanes properly for the break, and it involves all five members of the team. It is also a good conditioning drill. The positions of the players around the circle may be changed so that they are drilled on all of the positions of the break.

Joe Fields—named "Coach of the Year" in FJCC Division II for the 1965–66, 1966–67, and 1967–68 seasons—has coached the Lake City Junior High Timberwolves for six seasons in which he has recorded 104 wins against 41 losses. Before this he was basketball coach for three seasons at Columbia High School in Lake City, Florida, where he won 58 games and lost 22. His team at Columbia was runner-up in the state. At Lake City Junior College he led his team to the runner-up spot in the State Junior College Tournament in 1967.

FAST BREAK SITUATION DRILLS

John Glading

Richmond Hill High School, New York, N.Y.

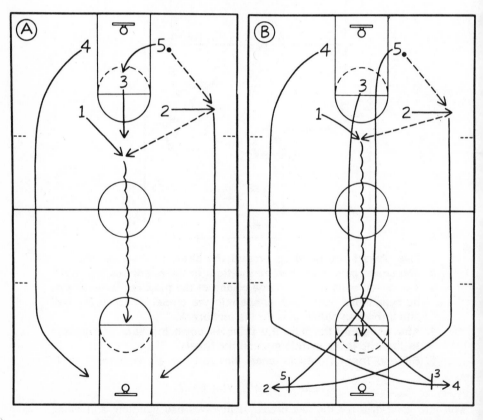

A. *Standard Three-Lane Break.* Player 1 always stops at the foul line for defense.

B. *Shot from the Corner with Pick from Trailer.* Allows regular pass to 4 or 2 or to trailers 3 or 5, plus the pass to 4 or 2 with a pick

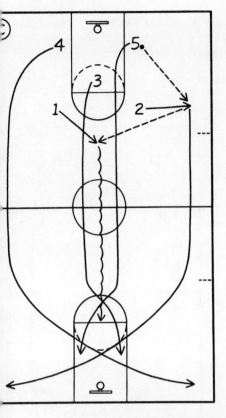

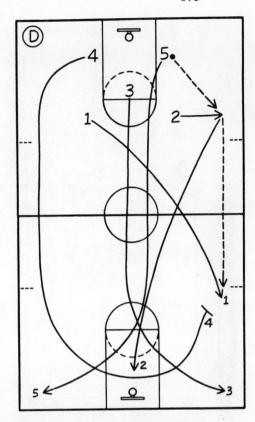

or screen from 5 and 3 for end line drive or protected jump shot.

C. *Feed to Trailer.* Same pattern except 1 feeds 3 or 5 on trailer. By calling "double," the first trailer through gives over-the-head pass to second trailer for layup.

D. *Short Court Break.* The short court break gives variety. This allows 1 to make scoring pass to 2, 4, 3, or 5. Player 1 may also drive or jump shoot off the #4 pick.

Special Value of the Drill

This series of fast breaks gives team unity but also allows individual initiative. The high lead pass is used 90% of the time for the layup except for the trailers.

John Glading began his coaching career at John Adams High School in New York City. In five seasons there his teams won 69 games and lost 21. While at John Adams High his teams made the New York City playoffs four out of five years. They had not been in the playoffs for over 20 years before he arrived. In 1961 he moved to Richmond Hill High School in New York City where he compiled 108 wins and 34 losses in eight seasons. While at Richmond Hill his teams made the New York City playoffs six out of the eight years.

Fast Break—Ball Handling Drill

Dan Glines

San Jose State College

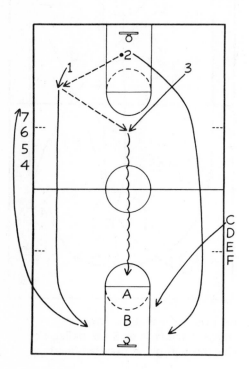 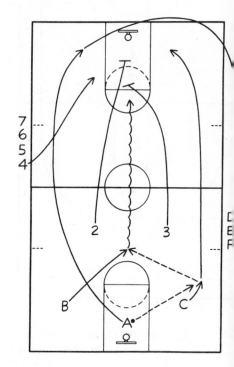

1-2-3 fast break against A-B. As soon as the group of 1-2-3 pass mid court, C runs on to the court to help A-B play defense. After a basket is made or after A-B-C gain possession, 1 drops out and goes to the end of the line on the side. 2-3 sprint back to play defense. A-B-C fast break the length of the court against 2-3. As soon as group A-B-C pass mid court, 4 runs onto the court to help 2-3 play defense. After the shot is made or 2-3-4 gain possession, A drops out and moves to the end of the line, while B-C sprint back to play defense.

The drill continues indefinitely. With a squad of 13 or 14 players, about 12-15 minutes is usually sufficient time for a workout. Each player drops out of the drill and returns to the end of the line at mid-court and waits his turn (in the order) to run on the floor. The drill may be used for warm-up at the beginning of practice and the time it is used will be reduced. It may be used at the end of practice and condition may be emphasized.

Special Value of the Drill

Even if a team does not employ the fast break, there are numerous fundamentals executed in the drill. For example, judgment decisions, excellent
passing, individual movement with and without the ball, shooting, offensive
and defensive rebounding (under game conditions) must be executed properly in this drill.

*Dan Glines began his coaching career at Acalanes High School were he
spent three seasons. His teams at Acalanes had a 55–24 record overall. In
1959 his team sported a 19–7 mark and a second place finish in the Tournament of Champions at Berkeley. His 1960 team finished with a 22–6
season mark, won the Foothill League title and took second place in the
Redding Acker Tournament. In 1961 he became the freshman basketball
coach at San Jose State College, a position in which he served for six seasons. In 1966 he accepted the head basketball job.*

CIRCLE AND GO DRILL

Dr. James Houdeshell

Findlay College

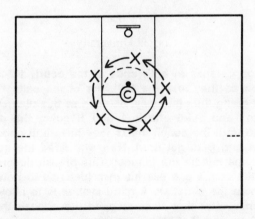

**Five players circle the coach, who has the ball. The players may also
be instructed to reverse direction to encourage agility. When the coach
throws the ball to the backboard, all five players attempt to rebound the
ball. After this rebound the five players fast break. The three-man lane
with two trailers is emphasized. Attention is given to the outlet pass, the
receiver's position for the outlet pass, how to fill the lanes, and the
coordination of the efforts of all five men to complete a successful break.**

Special Value of the Drill

1. Players must go to the ball (rebound).
2. All players must rebound.
3. A good way to keep many players active in team units.
4. Teaches all elements of fast break game.
5. Players like the drill.
6. Conditioning values.

In 15 seasons as head basketball coach in Findlay College, Dr. James Houdeshell has compiled a record of 197 wins against 130 losses. Before taking over the Findlay coaching helm in 1955, he taught at Lafayette-Jackson School in Allen County, 1953–54, and Findlay High School, 1954–55. Dr. Houdeshell has served as President of the Mid-Ohio Conference and Chairman of the Basketball Games Committee for the U.S. Collegiate Sports Council. He is also a member of the NAIA Ratings Committee and All-American Selection Committee. He has served as President for the NAIA Basketball Coaches, and has been a member of the NAIA National Tournament Committee. Seven times his teams have participated in the NAIA Small College Playoffs, and he has led two teams to the National Tournament in Kansas City.

11-Man Fast Break Drill

Jerry Lace

Cornell University

A and B stay on defense at both ends of the court. 1-2-3 will attack A and B. As soon as they lose the ball, the coach calls "go" and 7-8-9 attack A and B going the other way. As soon as this play ends, the coach again calls "go" and 4-5-6 attack A and B going the other way. A-B stay on defense until the coach thinks they have had enough. It will not take long for A and B to get tired. Men who need the conditioning are usually kept in the middle the longest. This breaks down to a three-on-two drill, and the coach can use his own ideas as to how he wants the defense to handle the situation. A good system is to allow the two men to get off defense after they have stopped the offense three times in a row. It makes them give that little extra effort.

Special Value of the Drill

1. It is an excellent conditioning drill. All 11 men are moving without any extended standing around.
2. Sets the defense against the break.
3. Gives practice in ball handling on an offensive advantage situation.

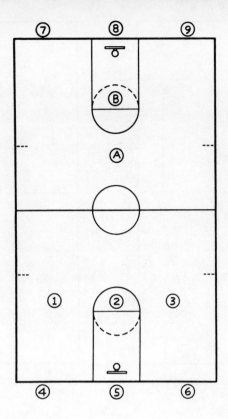

4. The drill pinpoints the men who need additional conditioning. It helps find the men who want to play through special effort on defense.

In 1968 Jerry Lace became the head basketball coach at Cornell University. He was in charge of the Big Red varsity soccer team and was a basketball coaching aide from 1963 through 1968. He served three years as freshman basketball coach and was the varsity assistant two seasons prior to assuming the top position. His yearling teams had a 29–10 record topped by a 14–1 mark in 1965–66.

THREE-MAN FAST BREAK DRILLS

Bruce Larson

University of Arizona

Full court and back. Passing only for five minutes.

Middle man always rebounds. The wing men cross underneath and start back after layup shot.

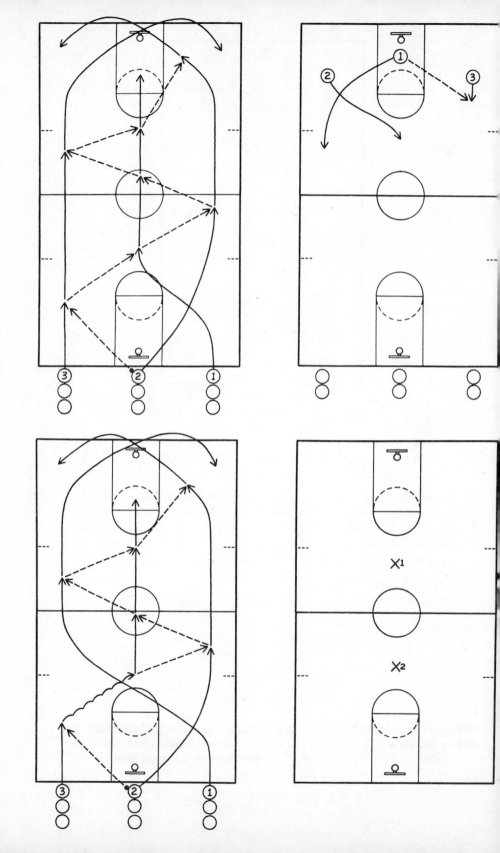

Dribble phase In this part of the drill the players assume the middle man is covered so 3 dribbles to the middle and then into the passing drill. The middle man goes to the side the dribbler came from.

Two defensive men are now added. This usually comes after the first week of practice. This helps wing man know whether he can pass to the middle or must dribble to the middle.

Special Value of the Drill

The drill teaches two fast break rules: (1) fill the middle from the weak-side, and (2) dribble to the middle if you can't pass to the middle. It also gives the players practice in passing at full speed and shooting at the end of the break. It's also an excellent conditioner.

University of Arizona's head basketball coach, Bruce Larson, began his coaching career in 1952 at Eastern Arizona Junior College. In 1957 his team was the National J.C. runner-up. After six years at Eastern Arizona he moved to Weber College, where he remained for two seasons. His team won the National Junior College Championship in 1959. In 1960 Coach Larson moved to the University of Arizona. After two years as an assistant coach, he became the head basketball coach in 1962. In nine seasons at Arizona he has compiled a record of 108 wins against 98 losses.

THREE-MAN FAST BREAK DRILL

Arad McCutchan

University of Evansville

The coach throws the ball against the board. Any one of the three men may rebound, after which a three-abreast fast break develops. The outside men should be within six feet of the sideline when they reach the free throw line extended. As many as five groups of three are kept fairly busy with the drill.

Special Value of the Drill

The drill emphasizes rebounding, passing, shooting, and quickness. It helps to teach the players to catch and pass the ball at top speed without dribbling.

Arad McCutchan gained recognition as one of the all-time greats of the University of Evansville and served as captain of the 1933–34 team. His 23-year coaching mark stood at 377 wins and 231 losses. He ranked 12th in the number of wins for active coaches in the nation. His most successful season was in 1964–65, when his squad finished an undefeated season with

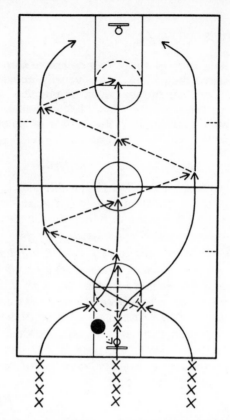

a record of 29–0. As a member of the Indiana Collegiate Conference, Coach McCutchan's teams have won ten championships and placed second three times in the last 14 years. His 1959, 1960, 1964, and 1965 teams were National Champions of the NCAA College Division. Coach McCutchan was honored as Coach of the Year by his NCAA colleagues in 1964 and 1965.

TEN-MAN DRILL
FAST BREAK OFF SUCCESSFUL OR UNSUCCESSFUL
FREE THROW DRILL

John Moro

Peekskill High School, Peekskill, New York

(Diagram 1)

Ten Man Drill. **Shooter A moves about and shoots from different spots on the floor. He then attempts to cut off the outlet pass. If unsuccessful,**

182

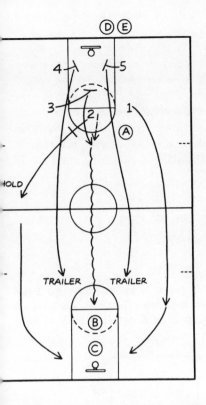

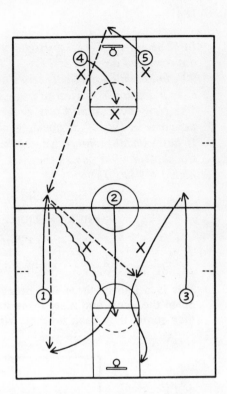

he drops back on defense with his two teammates (B and C) who are already set up in tandem defense under the opposite basket. To save time D and E are waiting for the team to come back the other way with the same drill. It is most important that all *five men* participate in the fast break because a *five*-man fast break, well executed and disciplined, will always catch one lazy performer who does not hustle back. The main rebounders (4 and 5) usually hit 2 at mid court or 3, the dribbler, at the top of the key. No matter who receives the outlet pass, the ball must end up with 3 in the middle. Every lane must be filled *exactly* as diagrammed. Each fast break man must be spread proportionately so that no one defensive man can cover two offensive men.

(Diagram 2)

Fast Break Off Successful or Unsuccessful Free Throw. The players line up as shown in the diagram. 5 retrieves, steps out, and tosses a baseball pass to either 1 or 3 coming back to meet the ball. Whichever side the ball is thrown, 2 heads for that corner. Now 1 has three options: (1) pass to 2 for quick jumper with rebounding by 3; (2) pass to 3 cutting across the middle of the court; or (3) a dribble to foul line for jumper or a pass to 3. There are several options but the basic one is diagrammed above.

In 12 seasons at Peekskill High School in Peekskill, New York, John Moro has compiled a record of 172–52. In the last five years his teams have won 90 games while losing only ten. They have won five consecutive conference championships in the last five years. In both 1967 and 1968 Peekskill won The New York State Class A sectionals. Peekskill averaged 82.6 points per game in 1968—the highest scoring high school record ever in the area. It has won 38 consecutive regular season games for a sectional record. Coach Moro was named the New York Daily News *Coach of the Year in both 1965 and 1968.*

FOUR-ON-THREE FAST BREAK DRILL

Clinton Morris

Broward Junior College

This is a four-on-three fast break drill. If Team A scores, they go back down the court and meet three defensive men from Team B. As long as they score, they keep the ball. When Team B or X gets the ball, all four

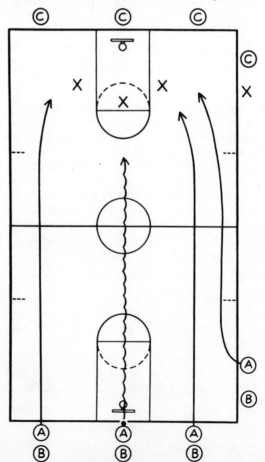

go on offense and keep possession as long as they are able to score. When a team is to go on defense, one man will step out of bounds until his team gets the ball, at which time he will come back on the court and join the four-man fast break.

Special Value of the Drill

The drill provides opportunities for practice in all the important aspects of play such as ball handling, shooting, rebounding, passing, and defense in addition to being an excellent conditioner. The players find it to be highly competitive and fun.

Clinton Morris began his coaching career at Woodall High School in Columbus, Georgia, where he recorded a 36–2 two-year mark. From there he moved to Greenwood High School in Greenwood, Florida, for one season and then to Carribelle High in Carribelle, Florida. In 1964 he was named head basketball coach at Broward Junior College in Fort Lauderdale, Florida. Since coming to Broward, Coach Morris has compiled a record of 75 victories against 50 defeats.

FIVE-ON-TWO DRILL

Stan Morrison

Freshman Coach, San Jose State College

The same two men (X) are used for five-minute periods before they are relieved. Usually they are guards although forwards and centers can be used. First string guards are used first, second string next, etc. The X's shoot the ball from anywhere—usually over the outstretched hands of one of the defensive guards (G). The big men (C and F's) rebound and start the fast break. The X's can do anything they want to stop the five fast-breakers—flood the outlet pass area, cheat, draw the offensive foul, get back in tandem defense, anything! After the fast break has culminated in either a basket or the X's gaining possession, the three big men (C and F's) spring back, with vision on the ball, to a position forming a line from sideline to sideline across the free throw line. An assistant coach can throw a variety of passes to any one of the three retreating big men. They are to catch the ball with two hands and stop without traveling or dribbling. Up court, the two X's take the ball out of bounds whether the basket was made or the ball rebounded. Once the inbounds pass is made, the two defensive guards (G) play tough pressure defense, forcing the ball to the helping defensive player, communicating with calls ("Help left," "Open," etc.). Double team situations can be incorporated into the drill if desired. When the X's get one dribble past half court, the three big men shout out "Normal" and the defensive G's back off into normal half court defense. Then five new men come onto the court and the X's put up another shot and the drill begins again.

Special Value of the Drill

1. It teaches blocking out by the defensive guards.
2. It teaches game-like reactions in fast breaking as adjustments are made to the gambling tactics of the X's.
3. It teaches ball handling and minimizes dribbling in fast break situations.
4. It incorporates good tandem defensive problems and forces communication.
5. It teaches players to retreat in a sprint with their heads over their shoulders and vision on the ball.
6. It teaches players how to catch the ball (interceptions) and keep balance and control.
7. It teaches how to pressure a dribbler and force him towards his weaknesses (left-handed speed dribble, etc.).
8. It teaches up court defensive communication in two-two situations.
9. Its outstanding feature is that it teaches players how to bring the

ball up court under great pressure and duress. The X's become greatly fatigued under the continued onslaught of the five fresh fast-breakers, whose poise and leadership are brought to the fore. The fast-breakers (all five) crash the board if their layup or jumpshot is missed and keep battling the two smaller X's until the shot is made or the X's rebound the ball. If the ball is stolen or turned over, the same five attack immediately from the spot on the floor where they gain possession. Every five minutes two new X's are brought out and the old X's are sent to the end of the G line.

Stan Morrison was a forward-center under Pete Newell during the California Bear's championship years. He was a sophomore the year the Bears won the NCAA (1958–59). He played for the last San Francisco Olympic Club team in 1962–63 while working on his teaching credential at Cal State Hayward and assisting Cal Coach Rene Herrerias with the varsity and junior varsity teams. After this he served as head man for the El Camino High School Eagles in Sacramento, California. In his last season El Camino won the co-championship of their conference. In 1966 he became the assistant basketball coach at San Jose State College.

FIVE-MAN FAST BREAK DRILL

Jerry Mosby

Blue Mountain College

This drill is used with five men in the diagrammed positions. Numbers 1 and 4 are forwards, number 5 is a center, and numbers 2 and 3 are guards. The coach throws the ball against the backboard; if it is rebounded by X1 he passes to X2 on his side of the floor. X3 breaks across the floor for the second pass behind the center line. X4 breaks down the floor when he sees the ball is rebounded by someone else. X5 replaces X1 and goes down the side of the floor. X1 replaces X5 and acts as the trailer down the floor. X3 hits either 4-5 or 1 for the layup. This may be run to the opposite side if X4 gets the rebound. If X5 gets the rebound, the first pass goes to the guard on his side of the court. This drill is used for two minutes and it is required that 12 baskets be made. The players run the number of laps short of this number. They must complete the second pass behind the center line and make at least three passes. If the ball goes out of bounds, they can't count it. They set up at each end after the basket and go to the opposite end of the floor.

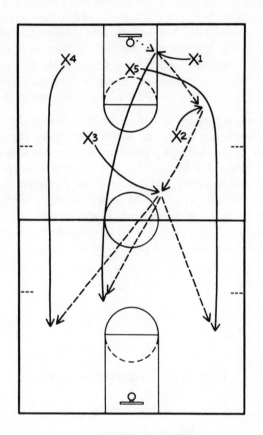

Special Value of the Drill

The drill gives players practice in forming a "cup" for rebounding, teaches them to get the first pass out quickly, develops good passing, and puts pressure on the layup. It is a good conditioning drill.

In 20 seasons of coaching, Jerry Mosby has compiled 320 wins for an average per season of 16. His career began at Eagle Point where he remained for four seasons. From there he moved to Newport where he also remained for four years. After one season at Lakeview, he spent five years at Astoria before becoming head basketball coach at Blue Mountain College in Pendleton, Oregon. His outstanding record includes several league and county championship teams. His teams have been frequent entrants in the state tournament. Since coming to Blue Mountain College his record stands at 85 wins and 34 losses,, and his team was Oregon Community College Champion in 1969.

Blitz Drill

Johnny Orr

University of Michigan

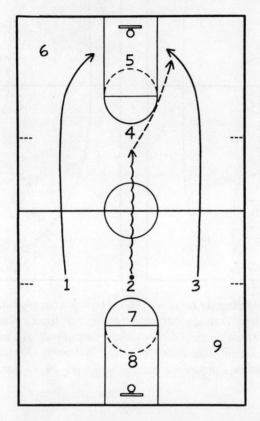

1, 2, and 3 run a three-lane fast break against 4 and 5. 4 and 5 rebound the missed or made shot and pass out to 6. 6 takes the middle, 4 and 5 fill the lanes and fast break against 7 and 8. 7 and 8 rebound the missed or made shot and pass out to 9. 9 takes the middle, 7 and 8 fill the lanes and fast break against X1 and X2.

Special Value of the Drill

This drill is a great conditioner. It is a good passing drill for outlet pass to start fast break, and it teaches the players to fill the lanes. It is an excellent drill for two men trying to stop the fast break. Good checking out and rebounding techniques must be used in the drill.

Johnny Orr, an outstanding football and basketball player at the University of Illinois and Beloit (Wisconsin) College, served as an assistant on the Wisconsin basketball staff and was head basketball coach for three seasons at the University of Massachusetts before moving into the head job at the

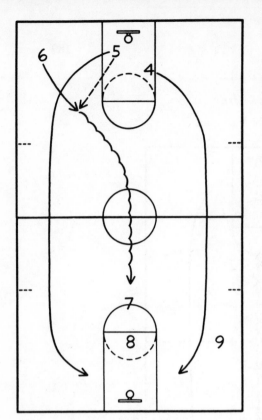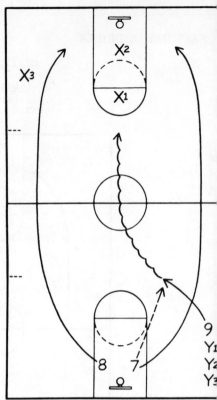

University of Michigan. In nine years of prep coaching at Milton High
in Wisconsin and Dubuque High in Iowa, his teams posted a 118–68
record in basketball and a 14–10–1 mark in football. He was an assistant
coach at Wisconsin four seasons before becoming Massachusetts head
coach. His Yankee Conference teams there were 29–15 for three seasons.

ALL-PURPOSE DRILL

John Rendek

Assistant Coach, Tulsa University

**As shown in the diagram, the coach puts the ball up on the boards.
Assume that X1 rebounds it. As he does, players in front of mid court
lines fill the outlet areas. X2 has two options—he can release the ball to
the player in the outlet area, or he can "kick-out" with it on the dribble.
If he releases to the outlet man, that man will dribble to the middle
break lane while the weakside outlet man floods outside lane on his side.
The rebounder fills the wide lane on his side. These three people attack**

190

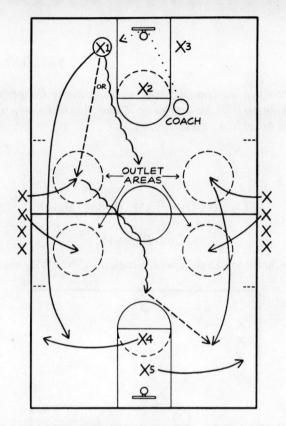

X4 and X5, the two defenders. This three-two situation will continue until the offense scores or the defense rebounds. If a goal is made, either X4 or X5 will grab the ball and the situation reverses toward the other end. If, for instance, X4 rebounds, then X5 will go in back of one of the sidelines and two of the three men who were on offense will remain on defense.

Special Value of the Drill

1. It creates a "game type" situation (three-on-two break).
2. It provides transition from one phase to another (offense to defense).
3. It covers all basic fundamentals of a sound running game: (a) rebounding, (b) outlet pass, (c) filling lanes.
4. It is very competitive.

John Rendek began his coaching career at Crofton, Kentucky, where he compiled a record of 70–17. From there he moved to Christian County High School in Hopkinsville, Kentucky. His record over a four-year period was 91 wins against 21 losses and included three district championships and one regional championship. Following this he coached at Louisville Male High School in Louisville, Kentucky. During his four years there he recorded 94 wins against 19 losses and won four district championships.

In 1968 he coached the United States All-Stars in the Dapper Dan Classic in Pittsburgh. After this he moved to Tulsa University where he is currently serving as assistant coach.

TWO-ON-ONE FAST BREAK DRILL

Lou Romano

Charleston High School, Charleston, West Virginia

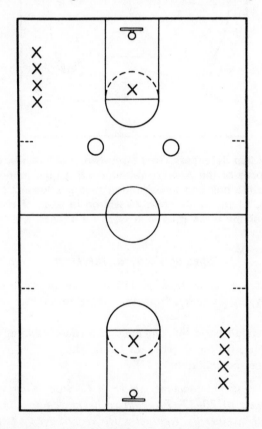

One man on defense tries to stop the two offensive men from scoring. After the shot is taken, X tries to get the ball on the rebound. If he gets it off the board, he passes out to the first man in the line at the free throw line extended and goes with him on the break to the opposite end of the court. The two men go against one man at the other end and the same procedure begins again. Every player has a chance on offense and defense. The men on offense shoot until they make the basket.

Special Value of the Drill

This drill provides practice in all the categories of play but it is especially valuable in teaching timing. It is run for 20 minutes every day in practice.

In eight seasons at Charleston High School in Charleston, West Virginia, Lou Romano has compiled an amazing 156 wins against only 28 losses. Coach Romano's teams won 48 straight games to tie the West Virginia Class A record. His teams lost a total of only three games in their last 75 contests. Coach Romano has recorded four Kanawba Valley Conference Championships during this time. In 1967 Charleston was the runner-up in the state championship and in 1968 they won the state crown.

TEAM FAST BREAK DRILL

Dave Strain

Rapid City High School, Rapid City, South Dakota

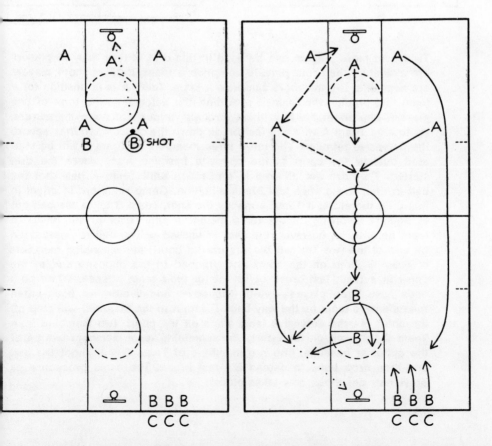

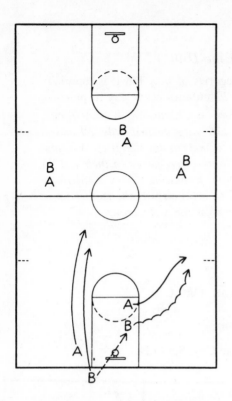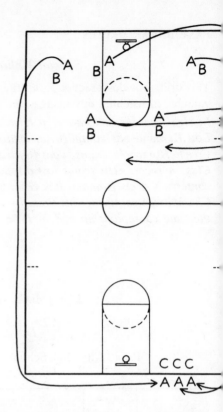

Twelve or more players can be used in this drill. If less than 15 players are available, then four players comprise a team. If 15 or more players are available, five members comprise a team. Team A is in position for a team fast break with Team B providing the defense in the form of two players who shoot the ball, then, through various defensive maneuvers, try to stop Team A who will fast break down the court when they secure the defensive rebound. The other three members of Team B will be situated outside the court at the opposite baseline from where the drill started. They are not allowed in the action until Team A has shot the ball in their five-on-two fast break situation. Game rules are in effect in this drill; therefore, if Team A makes the shot, Team B takes the ball out of bounds involving all the team members and Team A will revert to team defense. If, however, the shot is missed or the ball is intercepted by one of the two Team B players on the court, the remaining members of Team B jump on the court and proceed to the opposite end of the court in a team fast break or to set up their team offense. When both ends have been played—five-on-two down and five-on-five back—then the defensive team on the way back (Team A in the diagram) will step off the court. As the defensive team steps off the court, two members from Team C will step on the court. The remaining team members will be at the opposite baseline. The two members of Team C will shoot the ball and then drop back to defend B's fast break. The same procedure as previously described now takes place.

Special Value of the Drill

1. Reaction from offense to defense with a fast break situation going to one end and proper reaction from offense to defense when the shot is made or the ball is intercepted.
2. Many times in just fast breaking drills, the ball handling becomes sloppy. In this drill the defense will turn mistakes by the offense into baskets. This makes it more game-like.
3. It is a good drill for working on the press or against the press.
4. Excellent drill for conditioning ball players without using a full-scale scrimmage.
5. Involves all squad members.
6. The coach can utilize this drill for offensive work against changing defenses by having each of the teams use a different defense. Therefore, you can have practice in different defenses and against different defenses.

Dave Strain began his coaching career at Deadwood High School in Deadwood, South Dakota. In three seasons his teams won the District 31 Championship twice. In 1962 he moved to Rapid City High Schoool in Rapid City, South Dakota, where during seven seasons he has compiled a record of 137 wins against 32 losses. His teams were Section VII Champions during six of those seasons. They were runners-up in the State "A" Tournament in 1964 and 1966. They won the State "A" Championship in 1969. During that season Coach Strain was named South Dakota Coach of the Year and was also selected as District VII Coach of the Year by the National High School Athletic Coaches Association.

THREE MAN FAST BREAK DRILL

Dean Smith

University of North Carolina

The players are divided into three lines. The ball starts on side 3. (More experienced players should use two balls in this drill.) The first pass is a chest pass to the middle man. The second pass is a chest pass back to the side. The third pass is a chest pass back to the middle man. The fourth pass is a bounce pass to the opposite wing man for a layup. The other wing man rebounds the shot. The fifth pass is an outlet pass to start the break. The sixth pass is a baseball pass to the end of the line. Then the man in the 2 line begins a new three-man fast break by passing to the middle lane. The same routine is followed again by the next three men.

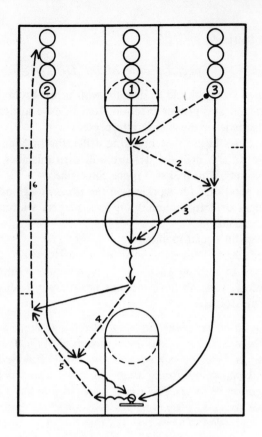

Special Value of the Drill

1. Excellent warm-up drill.
2. Incorporates all types of passes.
3. Layup practice.
4. Fast break organization.

Dean Smith's eight-year Tar Heel record is 147 wins against 60 defeats. He has guided the Tar Heels to an unprecedented three straight championships in the Atlantic Coast Conference and Eastern Regional Tournaments. Carolina finished second in the nation in 1968 and was fourth in both 1967 and 1969. In those three years, North Carolina won 81 games while losing only 15. Coach Smith's teams have captured 45 of their last 51 games in the Atlantic Coast Conference which is considered one of the toughest leagues in America. He came to Carolina in 1958 as an assistant to the successful Frank McGuire, who only two years before had guided the Tar Heels to an unbeaten season and the national championship. Coach Smith's first team, caught with mediocre talent, had an 8–9 record, the only losing mark of his entire regime. Carolina was 15–6 in 1963, 12–12 in 1964, 15–9 in 1965, 16–11 in 1966, 26–6 in 1967, 28–4 in 1968, and 27–5 last campaign.

Continuous Action Fast Break Drill

Donald Smith

Bucknell University

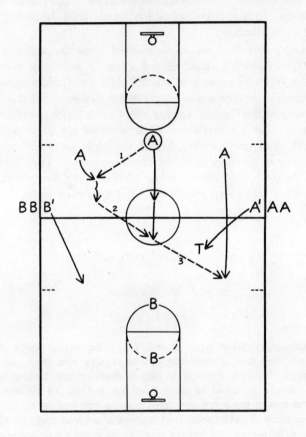

Divide the squad into two groups, A and B. Three players from Team A approach in straight lanes against Team B's two defensive men. When Team A advances to the top of the foul circle, A1 adds the trailer option while B1 provides a third defensive position. There is a momentary three-on-two situation, then the four-on-three situation. On a defensive rebound or field goal situation, the two wing men from Team A assume the defensive positions beyond half court. The middle man and the trailer from Team A challenge the in-bounds pass, or following a defensive rebound, they may double team the rebounder or challenge the outlet pass. When Team B completes the in-bounds pass or the outlet pass, the middle and trailer men from Team A move off the court to fill the next position. We place a time limit for the offensive unit to work for a shot.

Special Value of the Drill

The drill serves as a great conditioner plus incorporating the basic fundamentals: defense, rebounding, passing, dribbling, etc. The defensive pickup may vary from full to half court. Another important value of this drill is the constant emphasis on making the transition from offense to defense. Since basketball is a continuous action sport, drills involving game-like actions are most effective.

Donald Smith's first Bucknell team finished tenth nationally in team defense, and the 1966–67 squad ranked 22nd in field goal accuracy with 47.6%. The 1968–69 team won the "Middle Five" championship of the Middle Atlantic Conference and established a new seasonal scoring record. Before coming to Bucknell in April, 1964, Coach Smith spent a highly successful ten years at Elizabethtown College where his teams won 135 and lost 84. His basketball teams achieved the most successful seasonal and overall records in the history of the cage sport there. The 1963–64 team won the 24-member Middle Atlantic Conference Championship with a 20–5 record and placed second in the NCAA Eastern finals.

Rebound, Pass, and Go Drill

John Wagoner

Chabot College

This drill can start either right or left and then switch sides after about five minutes. The drill should start with layups and then, after several times through the line, change to the 12-foot or the 15-foot jump shot. Two balls should be used to speed up the action. X1 dribbles the ball to about the top of the keys and then passes the ball to X2 for the layup or the jump shot. X1 rebounds and throws a leadout pass to X2 who becomes the dribbler on the return trip. X1 becomes the shooter and the action is repeated at the west end of the court.

Special Value of the Drill

This is a great continuity drill. It combines dribbling, passing, layups at full speed, jump shooting, and the leadout pass to start the break.

In 1959 John Wagoner became the head basketball coach at Shafter High School where he recorded 37 wins against 25 losses. His teams won league championships in 1961 and 1962. The next year he moved to Chabot College where he is currently serving as basketball coach and chairman of the P.E. Department. His record at Chabot through eight seasons is 109–87. Since moving to a new campus in 1965, his teams have won 79 games and lost only 36. They were league champions in 1967–68.

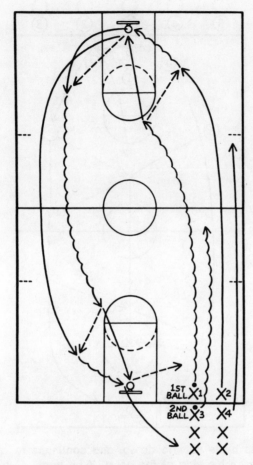

FIVE-MAN FAST BREAK DRILL

Fred Winter

University of Washington

#1 tosses the ball high on the board. #4 and #2 storm him once he has touched the ball. They two-time him and try to prevent him from getting the first pass out. Once he is able to get the pass by these men they become offensive teammates; this stimulates the condition of #1, #2, and #4 (front line defensive men) rebounding to the boards. #3 and #5 fill the outlet zones. #1 passes to either #3 or #5. All five men race for the three lanes. The forwards #2 and #4 come out on the sides they are rebounding. #3 and #5 fill the outlet zones and get themselves open for the pass from #1 (or from the rebounder). #5 should get to the top of the circle vicinity about five strides ahead of #1 (who always comes out the middle). Thus, #5 has established himself as the middle man. #3 passes

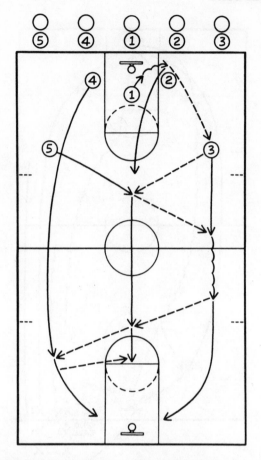

to #5 as soon as he is able to do so, and continues to race down the floor in the lane on his side of the court. If he beats #2 to this lane, #2 holds up and becomes a trailer. If #2 wins the race for this line, #3 holds up and becomes a trailer. #4 breaks down the court as shown and should fill this lane before #1 can cut over into it. If, however, #1 can fill this lane first, he does so. The forwards can generally beat the center to the wing lanes. Therefore, the center becomes a trailer by holding up and trailing the middle lane by 15 feet. #2 trails the left wing and moves over to trail #1 by a similar distance. #2 has defensive balance responsibilities and should not let any opponent get behind him. #1, the center, has the rule to go always to the offensive basket. If the first wave men hold up at the designated areas 15 feet apart, the secondary phase of the fast break develops.

Special Value of the Drill

The drill teaches players to execute the skills at a fast break pace and to use speed with control. Speed becomes a liability rather than an asset unless it is controlled. There is no better way to teach and to improve on con-

trolled speed than through fast break drills. Improved speed in the player
is reason enough for teaching the fast break.

*Fred "Tex" Winter became the head basketball coach at the University of
Washington in 1968 after a very successful tenure at Kansas State University and at Marquette University. His coaching career began in 1947 as
an assistant basketball coach at Kansas State University. After four years
there he went to Marquette University for two seasons as head coach. In
1953 he returned as head coach to Kansas State where he compiled a record of 262 wins against 117 losses. His teams at Kansas State won eight
conference championships, two NCAA Midwest Regional Championships,
and qualified for the NCAA playoffs six times. In 1959 Kansas State was
Number 1 on both major polls. In 1958 Coach Winter was named NCAA
Coach of the Year and the National Coach of the Year. He was four times
Big Eight Coach of the Year. He was named the NCAA Olympic Trials
Coach in 1968.*

REBOUND AND FAST BREAK DRILL
Dr. George Ziegenfuss
San Diego State College

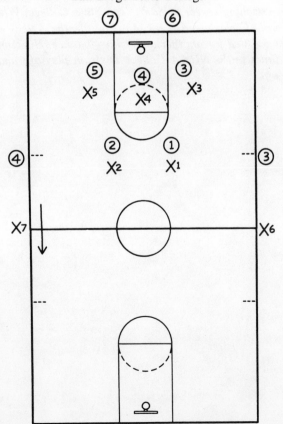

There are three men on offense and three men on defense (who also rebound). Two guards and one or two rebounders go on fast break. Only two men are back on defense and they vary positions. Two swing men fill in for rebounders who go on fast break. The swing men save time and provide rest for two rebounders who go on break. O3, O4, and O5 rebound a shot by the coach and get the ball out to O1 or O2 and go on break. X1 and X2 play defense against the break. O3 and O4 go in on next series as do O6 and O7. X6 and X7 come in as next defensive unit.

Special Value of the Drill

The drill approximates game conditions. It involves all squad members. There are not many interruptions. The drill covers a variety of skills on a specialist level.

In 21 years at San Diego State College, Dr. George Ziegenfuss has recorded 306 wins and 214 losses for a winning percentage of .566. His overall college record is 320–224. Coach Ziegenfuss started his coaching career at Bainbridge High School in 1940, where he remained two years. The next year he served as basketball coach at Whitman College in Walla Walla, Washington. From 1946 to 1948 he was assistant coach at Columbia University where the Lions won two straight Ivy League titles. In 1948 he began his coaching career at San Diego State College. While a member of the California Collegiate Athletic Association, the Aztecs won four conference titles and tied for another under his guidance. His teams have competed three times in the NCAA College Division play-offs and twice in the NAIA play-offs.

10

Combination Drills

Most drills offer an opportunity to work on more than one specific skill at a time, but because they stress a particular area of play, they may be easily categorized. Some drills, however, are very difficult to categorize because they do not identify a major area of stress. The following drills place a major emphasis on more than one aspect of play and are presented to the reader for use in any manner he deems advisable.

CIRCLE BALL

John Abramczyk

Murphysboro High School, Murphysboro, Illinois

Circle Ball. This drill may be used indoors or outdoors. If it is used in pre-season work out of doors, two circles (approximately seven feet in diameter) should be marked on the ground. The distance between the circles may be up to 100 feet, depending on the number of players. Indoors, the bottom halves of the two free throw circles may be used. No boundary lines, as such, are recognized. A basketball is the only piece of equipment required. To add variety or to work on developing strength, however, a weighted ball may be used, or ankle weights strapped on the participants. The number of players may vary depending on the space available, generally four to nine players on a side. Outside,

203

a large number of players may be involved, whereas indoors the space is limited and a smaller number of participants fits the situation much better. Teams are divided equally and each squad plays a tight man-to-man defense keeping alert for trap situations when a double-team may be employed. Play is commenced at the center of the playing area with a center jump. Players advance the ball toward their scoring circle only by utilizing the pass. Many situations will arise where the player will have the opportunity to work on all of the various passes—chest, bounce, hook, shovel, overhead, baseball, and even the behind-the-back pass. The ball may not be dribbled, and official basketball rules governing traveling are adhered to. One point is scored each time a player catches a pass in his scoring circle; however, a player may not just stand in his circle waiting for the ball. The three-second lane violation rule is applied to the circle. After a score is made, the player catching the pass places the ball on the floor in the circle; an opponent returns the ball into play with a throw-in from the circle and that team now advances the ball up the playing area toward their scoring circle. Penalties:

1. Dribbling the ball or traveling violation=loss of ball. The ball is placed on the floor by the guilty player, to be played at that point by his opponent.
2. Incomplete pass or fumble (not touched by a defensive player)= loss of ball. The ball is brought into play by an opponent. A deflected pass by a defensive player, ball knocked out of an offensive player's hands, or a loose ball=free ball; it may be picked up and played by either team.
3. Player standing in his circle longer than three seconds=loss of ball; play is resumed when an opponent plays the ball at the spot it was placed when the violation was called.
4. Offensive player with ball closely guarded by an opponent for five seconds=jump ball; ball is tossed up between the two players involved at that spot on the playing area.
5. There will be contact in this activity, particularly around the scoring area; fouls may be handled according to the method of officiating that they will encounter during the season; if the coach is attempting to develop a degree of aggressiveness, the contact may be ignored if the player fouled is not put at a disadvantage or if the foul is not flagrant.

For fouls the coach determines the penalty. The offending player may be required to leave the game and not be substituted for, thereby placing his team at a disadvantage, until a score is made. From personal experience, the boy thus expelled from the game is not gaining the values being sought in the drill, so an after-drill or after-practice penalty has been found to work out most satisfactorily.

A vigorous workout can be achieved in a short period of time; a brief, spirited five-minute game will not cause players to lose interest in the drill and will leave them "hungry" for the next encounter.

Special Value of the Drill

The values derived from this drill, besides conditioning, are the various skills that are so necessary to play basketball effectively: ballhandling, passing (dribbling is sometimes overworked in games), looking for an open man quickly, moving the ball swiftly, full-pressure defense, reacting offensively to pressure, out-maneuvering an opponent when a teammate has possession of the ball (faking, feinting, etc.), use of basketball rules in some instances (throw-in, traveling, three-second lane rule, five-second closely guarded rule, etc.), quick changes in the direction of the play (such as you have in a regular basketball game), aggressiveness on the part of the players in going for loose balls (since boundary lines are not present, the one who puts out the most gets the ball), and the one benefit that is extremely important—*teamwork*. As there is no "star" in this game, this drill teaches the importance of teamwork—the more all of the players on a team are utilized, the better are their chances of succeeding.

John Abramczyk began his coaching career at Shawneetown Junior High School in Shawneetown, Illinois, where, during two seasons, he compiled 34 wins against eight losses, a conference championship in 1962, and fourth place in the State Tournament during the same year. In 1963 he moved to Stronghurst High School in Stronghurst, Illinois, and recorded 77 wins and 14 losses while winning four consecutive conference championships from 1964 to 1967. Following this, he won 49 games while losing only nine at Schlarman High School in Danville, Illinois. In six seasons of high school basketball coaching he compiled a record of 126–23 and six conference championships. He recently accepted the head basketball job at Murphysboro High School in Murphysboro, Illinois.

FLOOR DRILL

Marvin Adams

Murray State College

To start the floor drill, #1 dribbles the ball with his outside hand to a point near the free throw line extended. #1 now passes to #2 moving to meet the ball from his sideline position, making sure the pass is in front and not behind him. #1 continues down the floor, timing himself for the layup or rebound position. #2 turns and passes to #3, making a cut from the opposite side of the floor. #2 continues on the court, cutting behind #3 to fill the outside weak lane. #3 passes to #4 who is moving into low post position and then continues his move across and down the floor

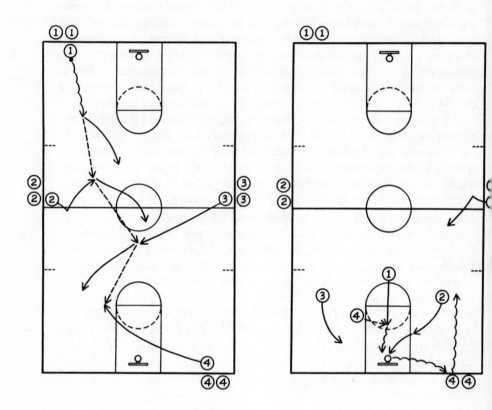

to fill the strong side breaking lane. #4 can pass or hand off to any of the three cutters for the layup. All lanes are filled. The middle cutter is usually used for the layup when first teaching the drill. Later any cutting lane can be used. When the rebound has been taken, the player recovering the ball will dribble with his outside hand (hand closest to the baseline) into the corner and hand off to a man in the #4 line. The player receiving the ball then makes his dribble up the sideline and the drill begins again in the other direction.

After an outstanding athletic career, Marvin Adams coached for three years in public schools before becoming head basketball coach at Murray State College in Tishomingo, Oklahoma. During three seasons at Murray, his teams have finished third and fourth in the National Tournament. In 1968 they won the Junior College NIT Championship held at Imperial Valley, California.

TWO-ON-TWO FRONTLINE POST PLAY

Ralph Barkey

University of California at Santa Barbara

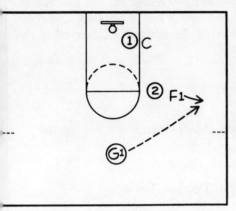 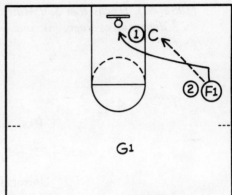

G1 (dummy G with no defense) throws a lead pass to F1 who has created a lead against pressure applied by 2 (defensive forward). F1 and C then play two-on-two against defense. Basic emphasis is on post play and subsequent moves that come from that operation. Defense will occasionally be adjusted, i.e. sag off the ball, which allows the offense to bring post man out to screen the defensive forward and roll to the basket. Heavy concentration is given to defense, i.e. active defense against the post, pressuring lead passes, defending the pass and cut situation, and screening out after shot is taken.

Special Value of the Drill

Major college success depends, by and large, on what is done in the basket area. This drill provides the following advantages:

1. Simulated game conditions that develop offense, defense, and board play.
2. Development of offensive and defensive post play: (a) how to establish an offensive post, (b) how to defend post play, and (c) how to run a forward-counter exchange.
3. How to pressure G-F lead passes. How to create lead against pressure: (a) forward-center exchange; (b) bring C high to "pig" defensive forward.
4. How to defense pass and cut and pick and roll situations.
5. Basic work on throwing lead pass, feeding a post man, feeding a cutter and screening off on the boards.

Ralph Barkey remained at the University of California at Santa Barbara after his graduation to serve as the assistant coach. He ultimately was rewarded the head job after a six-year stint as an assistant which was interrupted when he took over the basketball reins at the College of San Mateo. While at San Mateo he compiled a 36–21 mark after inheriting a basketball record that had seen the Bulldogs win just ten games in the preceding two seasons. He led them to an excellent 22–9 record his last season there (1962–63). It was that San Mateo club which ended up with a sparkling 49.7 defensive average, just one point off the national J.C. record at that time.

PASS AND PIVOT DRILL

Leon Black

University of Texas at Austin

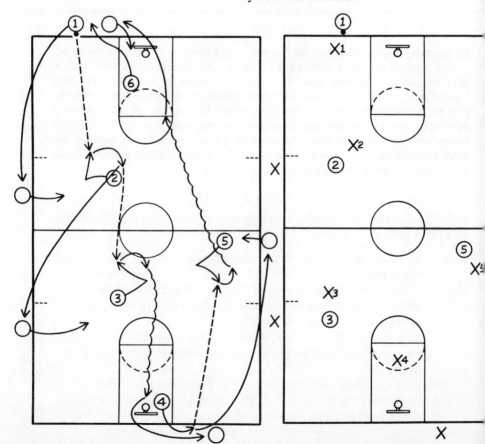

(Phase 1) **(1)** takes the ball out of bounds and **(2)** clears himself for the pass from **(1)**. When **(2)** catches the ball he is live on both feet and pivots to open up the middle of the floor, facing the imaginary defense. **(3)** clears himself and repeats the pivot action, except that he fakes and drives for the layup or jump shot. **(4)** rebounds and the action continues. **(5)** has no one to pass to as he makes the pivot so he dribbles for a jump shot or layup. **(6)** continues the action as described for **(4)**. Each player in the drill follows his pass to the next station. Additional players are positioned outside the playing area, preparing to take their position on the floor. Teaching points:

1. Timing of the pass at the moment the teammate is open.
2. Method of clearing for pass. Learn to play without the ball.
3. How to meet all passes and method of catching the ball "live" on both feet.
4. Teaching proper use of pivot and step fake.
5. What pass to use in each situation regarding distance—chest or snap pass. Make a chest pass when it can be accomplished. When distance is great enough to prevent this, make a baseball pass. The drill is also important in teaching proper dribble in a fast break situation.

Special Value of the Drill

This is an excellent warm-up drill, and it combines many teaching points. One aspect of basketball it prepares the players for on a daily basis is the attack of the press. If they learn to pass the ball when a man comes open, and always to pivot and face the defense prior to dribbling, they can successfully attack any press.

(Phase 2) A defense is now inserted in all spots. The defense is instructed to go full speed—to cover until the ball is dribbled, then release and move to the next station. The players go from defense to offense to the next station. They are now being taught defense on the full floor, one-on-one.

When **(1)** makes the pass to **(2)**, X1's defensive job is over and X2 defends on **(2)** until **(3)** can clear himself for the pass. When **(3)** catches the ball, X3's defensive assignment is over. As **(3)** dribbles toward the basket X4 moves forward to take **(3)** one-on-one. We now have **(3)** vs X4 in a one-on-one game and **(3)** converts from offense to defense on his shot. X4 rebounds the missed shot or gets the made shot out of the net. **(3)** pressures him on his pass to **(5)**. This continues to the other end of the floor with **(1)** becoming X1 and taking **(5)** one-on-one. **(5)** converts to defense on his shot.

Leon Black entered the coaching profession at Schreiner Institute in Kerrville, Texas. From there he moved to Van High School. In two years there he coached the Vandals to a 45–17 record. He followed with five remarkable seasons at Lon Morris Junior College (1960–1964), where his teams posted an outstanding 131–35 record. He then moved to Texas where he served as an assistant for three years before assuming the head coaching reins in 1967. His first year at Texas he led the 'Horns to an 11–13 record against stiff competition, and wound up going to the last game of the year before losing a one-point decision which knocked the Longhorns out of a tie for the conference title.

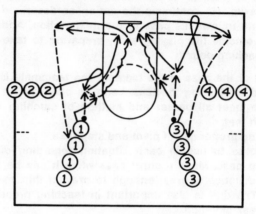

PIVOT AND GO DRILL

Bob Buck

Dodgeville High School, Dodgeville, Wisconsin

Numbers 1 and 3 have the ball. Number 2 runs out and touches the lane, pivots, and comes up to receive a pass from Number 1. Number 4 touches the baseline, pivots, and comes up to receive a pass from Number 3. Both 1 and 3 receive return passes and drive to the basket for a layup. After 1 and 3 shoot they go toward the sideline in their half of the court. 2 and 4 follow the shot and outlet pass to the shooter. After receiving the outlet pass, 1 and 3 pass to the man at the head of the line from which they started and the sequence begins again.

Special Value of the Drill

Because the drill incorporates quickness, agility, and coordination, it is extremely valuable in the development of a good fast break.

Bob Buck, the author of the book Shuffle and Press Offense for High School Basketball *(Parker Publishing Company), became head basketball coach at Dodgeville High School in Dodgeville, Wisconsin, in 1968 after serving as assistant coach to the late John Wilson. During Coach Wilson's tenure, he recorded 359 wins against 141 losses, including seven championships, one WIAA runner-up, and one WIAA State Championship in 1964. In his first season as head coach, Bob Buck led his team to the league and district championship while recording 18 wins against three losses.*

ONE-VS-TWO

Donald Burns

New Haven College

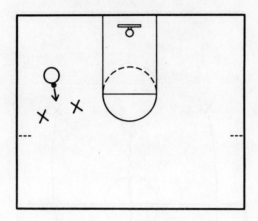

The man on offense tries to bring the ball up court and score against two defensive men. As long as he is able to score, he will keep the ball, going from end to end. When the ball is lost, the defensive man recovering it goes on offense. The man who had been on offense now plays defense with the other defensive man. The man who scores five baskets first, wins.

Special Value of the Drill

1. Teaches the techniques of two-man trapping on defense.
2. Gives practice to one offensive man bringing the ball up against two defensive men.
3. Gives players practice in shooting when tired and under pressure.
4. Emphasizes getting back on defense.
5. Is a great conditioner, particularly in early season.

Donald Burns begin his coaching career in 1961 at East Catholic High School in Manchester, Connecticut. In seven seasons he compiled an amazing record of 124 wins against 18 losses. His teams were twice State Champions, and were State runner-ups on a third occasion. In 1968 he accepted the head basketball post at New Haven College in West Haven, Connecticut. His team recorded 22 wins against only three losses, including four tournament victories and a District 32 Championship, during his first year.

Team Fast Break Drill

Larry Costello

Milwaukee Bucks

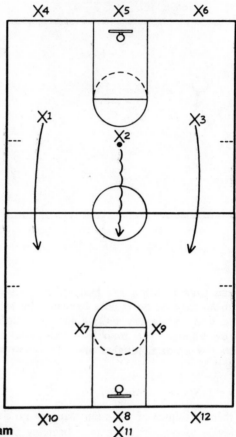

X1-X2-X3=1 team
X4-X5-X6=2nd team
X7-X8-X9=3rd team
X10-X11-X12=4th team

**No limit to the
number of participating
teams.**

The drill starts as a three-on-two fast break with X1, X2, and X3 advancing the ball up court. After the ball passes mid court, the offensive team is allowed one pass in an attempt to score on any two members of the X7, X8, and X9 team. After *one* pass is made, the third member of the defensive team comes on court to make it a three-on-three situation. If the offense scores, they are entitled to one point. As soon as one of the defensive men obtains possession, the team of X7, X8, and X9 will advance the ball to the opposite end of the court to challenge two players from the team of X4, X5, and X6. The coach can make the drill competitive by declaring the first team to score seven points the winner and making all the losers run laps.

Special Value of the Drill

The drill employs many basic fundamentals of play such as running, ball handling, passing, shooting, blocking out, and defense. It helps players learn to think and react.

In 12 years as a professional basketball player, Larry Costello built a reputation as one of the finest competitors in the game. He averaged 12.2 points a game in the NBA and might have gone on playing a while longer but for the opportunity to start a career in coaching. His best years as a scorer were in 1957–58, 1958–59, and 1960–61 when he averaged 14.9, 15.8, and 14.5 respectively. Always one of the league's leading free throw shooters, he made 2432 of 2891 from the line over the years for an .841 percentage. An NBA All-Star six times, Larry played on teams that missed making the playoffs only twice in his 12 years in the league. He spent two years with the Philadelphia Warriors, six years with the Syracuse Nationals, and four years with the Philadelphia 76'ers. A graduate of Niagara University, he was named to the Small College All-American Team in 1952–53 and in 1953–54.

COMPETITIVE "NUMBERS" DRILL

Dean Craig

Lakeview High School, Winter Garden, New York

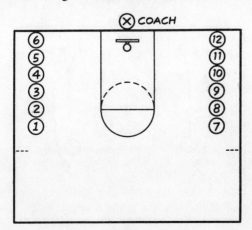

The coach numbers the players 1 through 12 and places half on each side of the court. He throws the ball anywhere on the court and calls out the numbers of two players. The player who retrieves the ball goes on offense against the other man until the basket is made, using the basket in front of the coach. For a variation, the coach can have the player on defense rebound the ball if the shot is missed and score a basket at the opposite end. Also, a two-on-two or a three-on-three can be used effectively.

Special Value of the Drill

1. It gives the coach an opportunity to evaluate his player's performances in early season practices.
2. It instills a lot of hustle in players (especially if they are divided into teams and the losers have extra duty).
3. It is a good conditioner (particularly using both ends of the court).
4. The coach may use the drill to evaluate fundamentals of play for each individual as a basis for future work. The drill is discontinued after the season is about three weeks old.

In 11 years of coaching, Dean Craig has recorded 139 wins against 135 losses at Lakeview High School in Winter Garden, New York. His teams have won two Holiday Tournament Championships, three district championships, one regional championship, and a runner-up in the state tournament.

SLIDE AND CHECK OUT DRILL

Johnny Dee

Notre Dame University

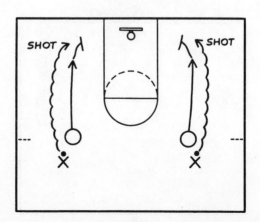

The squad is broken into two groups, each working at one of the main baskets. The group forms two lines, one at each guard position. One ball is used in each line. The offensive player drives to the basket by going outside. The defensive player slides down, preventing the opponent from getting a layup. The defensive player must step into opponent when he shoots and then check him out. Then he must get the ball. Only one line at a time operates at a basket. The lines alternate. Players switch lines after a turn.

Special Value of the Drill

OFFENSIVE VALUE

1. Player must execute driving move to outside from both sides. When going left he must dribble with left hand and he must use the right hand on the right side. He can execute rocker step, cross over, etc. for outside drive.
2. Player must shoot with left hand from left side and right hand from right side even if shot is not a layup.

DEFENSIVE VALUE

1. Player must slide down and out to prevent opponent from turning corner. He must get outside opponent to prevent him from moving in straight line to basket.
2. He must step into shooter on shot other than layup, and defend shot with outside arm (arm nearest baseline). Left-handed shot is taken—defender should have raised his right arm.
3. After stepping in and defending shot, he must check opponent out by means of reverse pivot and get the ball.

John Dee's pre-Notre Dame basketball coaching background includes four seasons as head coach at Alabama (including a Southeastern Conference Championship on the strength of an undefeated team), one title and three second-place finishes as coach of the Denver Truckers in the National Industrial League, and a year at the helm of the American Basketball League leading Kansas City Steers of the now defunct ABL. In his first five seasons at Notre Dame (including bids to the NCAA Tourney in 1965 and 1969 and a third-place finish in the National Invitational Tournament in 1968), Coach Dee has accumulated a 75–63 record. His nine-year collegiate coaching record is 143–88.

Gerald Duffy

Caribou High School, Caribou, Maine

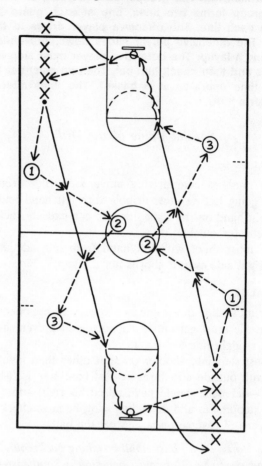

Two lines of players are stationed at each end of the court and on opposite sides. The first player in each line starts the drill by passing the ball to O1. He receives a return pass from this man and in turn passes to O2 stationed at center court. He again receives a return pass. This is followed by a pass to O3, a return pass from him, and a layup. After the shot the man moves to the end of the line at the opposite end of the court from which he started.

Special Value of the Drill

This is a great passing drill and also a great pass catching drill. Its conditioning value is excellent along with teaching players the skills involved in shooting a layup. When it is used for ten minutes a day it will show how the players can pass, move, and shoot when they are tired. It pays off at the end of the ball game.

*Gerald Duffy began his coaching career at Sherman High School in 1958.
During four seasons his team won 49 games while losing 21. During the
1961–62 season his team won the Katahdin Valley League Championship.
In 1962 he moved to Limestone High School where he compiled a record
of 42 wins and 30 losses, including Northern Aroostook League titles in
1964–65 and 1965–66. In 1966 he became the basketball coach at Caribou High School in Caribou, Maine. During three seasons he recorded 35
wins against 25 losses. His 1968–69 team was Maine State Champs.*

Combination Drill

Jerry Dugan

Lee High School, Huntsville, Alabama

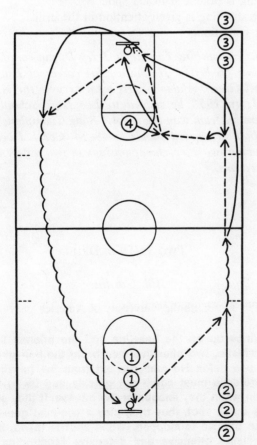

O1 throws the ball off the side of the board and rebounds the ball with good form. He then makes an outlet pass to O2 who is breaking up the floor. O2 takes a couple of dribbles if necessary and then passes the ball to O3 who is breaking up to meet the pass. O2 should go outside of O3 to the goal for a layup. O3 pivots to the inside and passes to O4. O4 makes a pass to O2 for the layup and follows the shot. O2 makes the layup and continues on back toward the other basket. O4 takes the ball out of the basket and makes a lead pass to O2 who receives the pass and dribbles to the other end for a layup. The player is penalized five pushups for one missed layup and ten pushups for two missed layups. Rotation: O1 goes to O4 line. O3 goes to O2 line. O4 goes to O3 line. O2 returns to O1 after shooting.

Special Value of the Drill

1. Gives practice in rebounding the ball high off the board and making a good outlet pass.
2. Gives practice in ball handling.
3. Pivoting is practiced in O3 spot.
4. Layup shooting is given attention in the drill.
5. Great conditioner.

In eight seasons of coaching basketball, Jerry Dugan compiled a record of 150 wins against 66 losses. He started his career at Hazel Green High School in Hazel Green, Alabama. His team became the AA State Champions in 1967. In 1958 he moved to Lee High School in Huntsville, Alabama, where his team won the AAAA State Championship. In two seasons at Lee High, his record stands at 48–14. Coach Dugan has the distinction of winning two state championships in two different classifications in successive seasons.

TWO-VS-TWO DRILL

Bill Gardiner

Catholic University of America

The defense lines up on the baseline and the offense lines up at mid court. At the whistle, two offensive men bring the ball quickly into scoring area and two defensive men run out from the baseline to stop the offense. The defense must come out quickly and be in the proper defensive position when they encounter the offense. If they stop the offense from getting a quick shot, they then play a two-man game until the shot is taken or the offense is stopped. When shot is taken, both groups go the boards utilizing offensive and defensive rebounding techniques. If

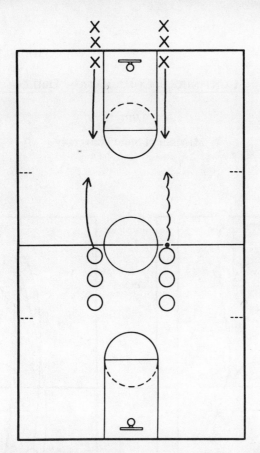

the defense rebounds, they spin out as they would on a fast break and, after one or two dribbles, they pass to a man in the offensive line with a two-hand chest pass.

Special Value of the Drill

The drill is valuable because the players learn to get into defensive position quickly. Players get both offensive and defensive rebounding practice, and spin-out practice for the fast break. The drill creates great attitudes for competitiveness.

For 13 years Bill Gardiner coached basketball at Spring Hill College in Mobile, Alabama, building the small school into a major basketball power in the South. His 1954 team won the Gator Bowl title, defeating both Florida and Georgia. In 1956 and 1957, Spring Hill won the Senior Bowl Championship, beating Clemson, Memphis State, Furman, and Morehead State. In 1959 he became head coach and athletic director at Loyola of New Orleans. From 1959 to 1966 his teams traveled coast to coast, playing some of the toughest schedules in the nation. Overall, Coach Gardiner has compiled over 325 wins as a college coach. He accepted the head basketball position at Catholic University of America in 1967. In two seasons his teams have recorded 25 victories.

Continuous Combination Drill

Joe Dan Gold
Mississippi State University

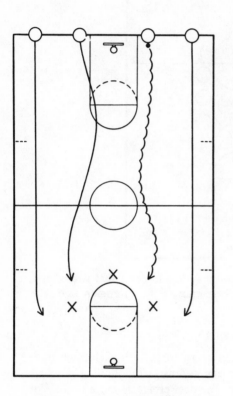 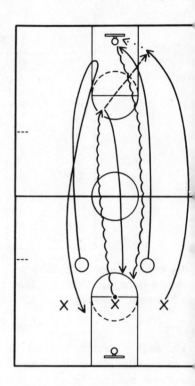

This drill combines four-on-three, three-on-two, and two-on-one situations for both offense and defense. Four men first go against three defensive men. When the defensive men get the rebound or when the offense scores, the three defensive men become offense and fast break against the two men in the middle lines from the group of four who were originally on offense. The two men from the outside lines go to the end of a defensive line. When the two defensive men rebound or gain possession of the ball, they fast break against the one middle man who was on offense against them. The two outside men from the group of three go the end of an offensive line.

Special Value of the Drill

The drill emphasizes both offense and defense. It also simulates game-like fast break situations.

Joe Dan Gold, one of the nation's youngest head basketball coaches at a major school, has completed four years as head basketball coach at Mississippi State University. He was elevated to the top position at State in March, 1964, succeeding the veteran James McCarthy, who is directing the New Orleans Buccaneers of the American Basketball Association. In Coach Gold's first two seasons, he directed his teams to identical 14–11 records. Before he became the head coach he served as freshman coach for two seasons at Mississippi State. During his two seasons he had a 22–3 record in 1963–64 and a 17–6 record in 1964–65.

UP AND DOWN DRILL

Jim Gudger

East Texas State University

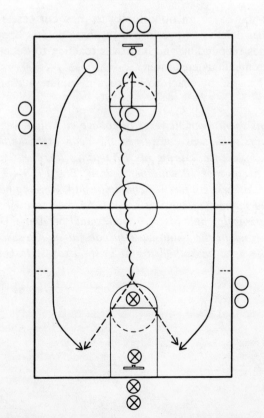

This drill is best suited for 12 to 15 men. Two big men and one guard are set in the right front court. There will also be two big men outside the end line waiting their turn. One guard will be outside the sideline at foul line extended waiting his turn. In the left front court two big men will assume a tandem defensive position. Two more big men will be outside the end line waiting their turn. Two guards will also be outside the sideline at foul line extended. The coach throws the ball against the board in the right front court to be rebounded by one of the two big men. The guard will step inside the foul line and call "ball." As they hit the guard the two big men must fill the lanes to the other end. They must step on the side line where the side line and center line intersect. As they go to the left front court they will be challenged by the two defensive men. Using the correct attack methods, the ball will be shot. As the ball is shot one of the waiting guards will run in inside the free throw lane and call "ball." The two defenders now become rebounders, pass the ball to the guard, and fill the lanes. Players waiting fill in appropriately and the action is continuous. The drill may also be used by having two guards fill into the sides and having the outlet pass go to sides.

Special Value of the Drill

1. Teaches big men to fill lanes quickly and react.
2. Teaches ball handling, especially as the fast break meets opposition.
3. Gives the coach an opportunity to pick out careless individuals.
4. Teaches defense as two men meet three on fast break.
5. Teaches rebounding and improves reaction to outlet pass.
6. Is a tremendous conditioner.
7. May be used by coach to improve discipline and attention to detail.

Jim Gudger has spent over 20 years in college coaching. While at Western Carolina University he was considered the dean of basketball coaches in the Carolina Conference. During his 19 seasons there, his teams won 342 games for an average of 18 wins per season. The 1958–59 team brought Coach Gudger his first conference championship, winning both the regular season and tournament crowns. His 1961–62 team brought another conference championship, and his 1962–63 squad won the District 26 title and placed second in the National Tournament in Kansas City. In 1968 he accepted the head basketball job at East Texas State University.

FOUR-ON-FOUR DRILL

Henry Iba

Oklahoma State University

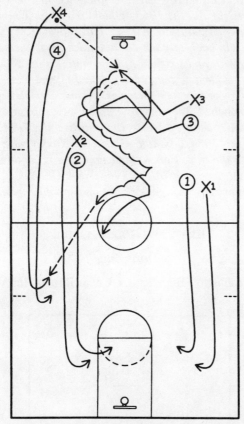

X4 has the ball out of bounds. The moves of X1, X2, and X3 may be controlled or they may be allowed to free-lance. When the ball is received in the court, everyone else clears out. A one-on-one is now created. Assume X3 has the ball bringing it up the floor. O3 has the job of stopping X3 and the other defensive men must keep their men from being receivers. The four men are directed to run the offense the coach desires. When the X's either score or lose the ball, the two groups of four reverse positions and bring the ball back up the floor in the same manner.

Special Value of the Drill

The drill helps both offensively and defensively. Four offensive men can be aligned in any manner the coach chooses. Most often they are aligned to meet pressure defenses.

In 1934 Henry Iba became the basketball coach at Oklahoma State University (then Oklahoma A & M) and was named Director of Athletics in the same year. 14 Missouri Valley Conference basketball championships or co-championships were won by Coach Iba's Oklahoma State teams before the school joined the Big Eight Conference in the spring of 1957. He won the Big Eight title in 1965. Oklahoma State University won the NCAA basketball championship in 1945 and repeated in 1946 (becoming the first school to win back-to-back NCAA titles); was second to Kentucky in the NCAA of 1949; and finished fifth or better in the NCAA four other times. Iba-coached collegiate teams have won 741 and lost 314 games. His OSU teams have recorded 629 victories against 291 defeats through 34 seasons. He has coached 39 years of intercollegiate basketball (after two years of high schol coaching). Hank Iba coached the USA Olympic basketball team for the 1964 Olympic Games at Tokyo where it won nine straight games and the title. For the first time, the USA Olympic Committee reappointed him as coach of the 1968 USA Olympic team in Mexico City and the team again won nine straight and the championship.

BEAT THE PRESS DRILL

Don King

Washington High School, Cedar Rapids, Iowa

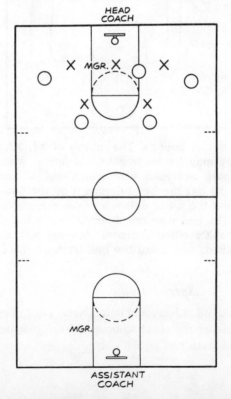

The assistant coach works with the O's who assume a basic offensive position to begin the drill. The head coach works with the X's who assume a defensive position to begin the drill. A manager is stationed at each end of the floor. The manager at the court where both teams begin starts the drill by making a layup. The O's immediately react to some full court press (predetermined by the assistant coach). The X's react immediately to their press attack and attempt to "beat-the-press." If the O's intercept, they attack the basket. If the X's beat the press, once they have scored or the play has ended at the opposite end, both teams assume the original positions ready to repeat the action in the reverse direction. On certain days, the X's work exclusively against the press. On other occasions the offensive and defensive roles are alternated in a sequence with the score being kept. The coach working with the pressing team usually uses and alternates two, three, or four different presses in one 15-minute session of this drill.

Special Value of the Drill

The drill gives the players confidence against any type of pressing defense. Our press attack is one of the first things we establish each season. Because of the flexibility of this drill, in the course of the season we have had a great deal of work against all types of presses and, in the process, have developed our own pressing game a great deal.

Don King has coached 18 years on all levels, from junior high school through college. He first attracted real attention in 1961 and 1962 at Nevada High School in Nevada, Iowa, where his teams compiled records of 20–2 and 22–2 and were rated in the Top Ten in Iowa despite being the smallest school in their group. He then coached four year at Coe College in Cedar Rapids, Iowa. His 1963 team led the Midwest Conference in offense. In the 1968–69 season his team at Washington High School in Cedar Rapids swept the Mississippi Valley Conference Championship with a 24–1 record, leading the league in both offense and defense. His team went on to win the Iowa State Championship. Coach King was named Mississippi Valley Conference Coach of the Year and District 2 (Big Ten States) Coach of the Year by the National Coaches Association.

EAGLE DRILL

Frank Layden

Niagara University

The two teams form a circle around the keyhole as shown in the diagram, usually wearing different colored shirts. Each man knows whom he is guarding, and they are probably better off if they are not next to each other in the circle. The coach, who is in the vicinity of the basket, will

shoot the ball to make or miss, will drop it, roll it, or throw it out of bounds as he desires. The teams will be running in a trot, and will not know when the coach's action will occur. The coach will then indicate which team he wishes to be on offense by calling out the color of the shirts as he begins the action with the ball. The other team will go on defense (coach specifies the type beforehand).

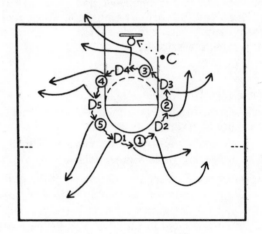

Special Value of the Drill

It teaches the players to change from offense to defense quickly, to pick up a man quickly, and to work together. The coach can check defensive position, individual speed, fulfillment of individual defensive assignments. He may blow the whistle at any time, freezing all ten players so that he may check the offensive team as well. It is a drill that can be organized quickly. It puts emphasis on good team defense while having the ability to check the individual's attitude and physical capabilities. It also is a valuable conditioner since a lot of running is involved.

Francis Layden returned to his alma mater Niagara University after a highly successful career as athletic director and basketball coach at Adelphi-Suffolk College in Oakdale, Long Island. Before this he coached at Seton Hall High School, Patchogue, where his full-court press was dubbed by sportswriters as "Layden's Monster Defenses." His best year was during the 1964–65 season when his Blue Eagles ended the season with a 21–3 mark. He left Seton Hall in 1966 to become athletic director and head basketball coach at Adelphi-Suffolk. His success there can be measured by the team's 13–5 record during the 1967 season.

Teams Competition Drill

Jack McMahon
San Diego Rockets

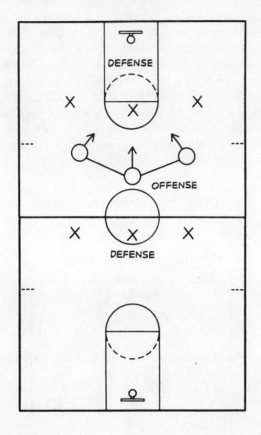

This is a combination offense and defense drill designed to take care of a situation in which the team is short a man or two in practice. Three teams of three men each are used: blue, gold, and skins. The team designated as defense waits at mid court to apply mid-court pressure on the offense. When they gain possession of the ball they attack the three men at the other end of the court. The ball is kept as long as a team keeps scoring. Fifteen baskets constitute a win. If there is a foul, both baskets must be made to have it count as a basket. All fouls are two shot fouls.

Special Value of the Drill

It is a competitive drill and one that comes close to game-like conditions. While waiting to go on defense at mid court, the three men can decide what they will do on defense and plan what they will work on offensively when they gain possession of the ball.

Completing his 16th season in professional basketball and eighth year as a head coach, Jack McMahon boasts an overall record of 272 victories and 255 defeats in regular season play for a .516 percentage. His coaching career started at Kansas City in 1961–62 with the then newly-formed Steers of the now defunct American Basketball League. He led the Steers to a 58–21 record and the only championship in the league. In 1963–64 he coached the Cincinnati Royals to their best record in NBA history, 55–25, to finish second in the Eastern Division. The Royals were second again in 1964–65 and third in 1965–66 and 1966–67 before he decided to head west and join the Rockets for their first season of NBA play. McMahon went into coaching after a successful playing career that included All-America honors at St. John's University in Brooklyn and eight years in the NBA.

PRE-GAME WARM-UP DRILLS

Ray Mears

University of Tennessee

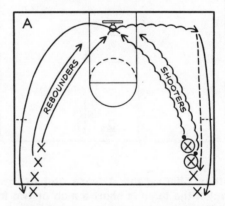

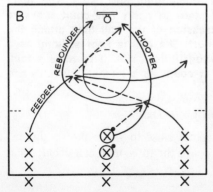

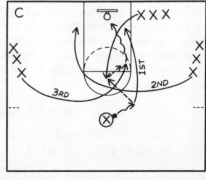

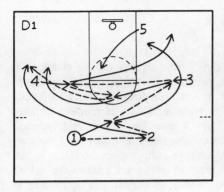
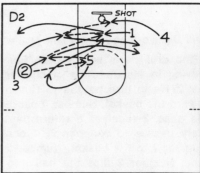

Drill A (Two-Guard Layup)

There are two lines, one on each side of the floor, with the first two men on the right side having a ball. The right side is the shooting side and the left side is the rebounding side. As soon as the layup has been taken, the rebounder pulls the ball out of the net and moves to the side quickly on a dribble. From this position he will square off and make a sharp baseball pass to the man at the head of the line on the right side. After the ball has been passed to the man in that line, both the shooter and the rebounder will sprint to the end of the line opposite from where they started.

Drill B (Three-Man Weave with Every Man Shooting Layup)

The ball always starts in the middle. On a weave, the player that makes the pass will go behind the receiver and continue in a course toward the basket. In this drill there is a shooter, a feeder, and a rebounder. They rotate in the following manner: feeder to shooter; rebounder to feeder; shooter to rebounder. As soon as the feeder makes the pass, he moves out quickly to the free throw line extended, getting set for his cut to the basket for his layup. When everyone has shot a layup, all three players move to the outside of the court and sprint to the end of the line, bringing the ball with them.

Drill C (Fancy Ball Handling with Three Cutters)

The ball will start at the point position with the three outside men passing the ball around sharply. The fourth man lining up underneath the basket will move quickly to the free throw line from which he will be ready to receive the pass. As soon as the pass is made from one of the outside men, he will start a ball handling routine, taking the ball around the waist, legs, and neck. At the same time the routine is going on, there will be three cutters criss-crossing off the post man. The man who makes the first pass to the middle will be the first cutter and the others will follow as a scissors pattern continues. The middle man will hand the ball off or make a bounce pass to the third cutter as he continues in for a layup.

Drill D (Five-Man Pepper Drill)

The drill starts with a pass from the 1 man to number 2. Number 1, moving in the direction of his pass, receives a return pass from Number 2. He in turn passes to Number 3 and cuts around him and heads toward the basket. Number 3 passes to Number 4 who is coming to meet the pass. 3 receives a return pass from 4 near the circle and immediately passes to Number 2. 4 continues across the court and follows Number 1 to the basket. Number 5 moves to a high post position in the lane. Number 2 flips the ball into 5 and receives an immediate return pass. 2 then passes to Number 1 and continues across the court and to the end of line 3. 1 now feeds Number 3 and cuts in front of him to the sideline and on out to the 2 line. 3 passes to 4 underneath for a shot and then moves on to the end of line 4. 4 shoots a layup under the basket and then goes to the end of line 5. The 5 man rebounds the shot and passes out to the man in line 1. 5 then goes outside the court and to the end of line 1.

Tennessee's Ray Mears has moved into the No. 2 spot on the list of all-time winningest basketball coaches. His 1968–69 Vols ended their season at 21–7, pushing Coach Mears' 13-year college coaching record to 250–75 and a win percentage of .769. The only coach now in front of Mears is Kentucky's veteran Adolph Rupp. The 1968–69 league record of 13–5 earned the Vols a second-place finish in the SEC. It continued their pattern of lofty conference finishes that began with second place in 1964 and continued with second in 1965, third in 1966, first in 1967, and second in 1968. This time the Vols earned a trip to the NIT in New York City where they finished third in a field of 16 teams. Coach Mears' use of sound defensive principles is revealed in the team's two national defensive championships in the past five years. His record at Tennessee follows closely the pattern he set at little Wittenberg University in Springfield, Ohio, where he won the NCAA College Division Championship in 1961, again primarily with tough defense. Ray Mears' Wittenberg Tigers finished tops in the nation four straight years in the category of fewest points surrendered.

THREE-ON-TWO

Ray Meyer

De Paul University

X1 comes up and stops (2) and X2 drops back in the middle and plays the first pass no matter where it goes. 2 passes to 1 and X2 takes him.

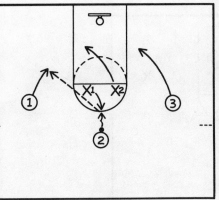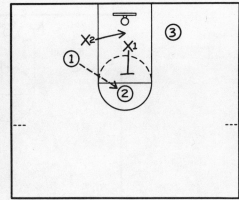

X1 turns and faces the ball as he slides back looking for a pass from (1) to (3). X1 must cut off the pass to (3). (1) passes back to 2 at the free throw line. X1 will come back and play 2 as X2 slides back in the middle. After the first pass to the side, the defense alternates taking the ball, while the other man goes under the basket. The offense is taught to keep the ball in the middle as they come to the circle. The middle man has more options this way. The middle man stops at the line and the wing men go inside and under. This drill is run the length of the court by placing a third line on the right out of bounds line. When the defense gets the ball, the man on the right joins in the three-man break. The drill combines offense and defense, running and ball handling, along with shooting and rebounding.

Ray Meyer arrived on the DePaul scene in 1942 after serving as Notre Dame's assistant basketball coach for two seasons. Immediately De Paul's reputation as an independent basketball power grew. Meyer took his team to the NCAA Tourney in 1943, a second-place finish in the 1944 NIT, and the NIT Championship in 1945. Despite the lack of outstanding talent, he has put his teams into six NCAA Tournaments and seven NIT Tourneys, and during his 26 years, Coach Meyer has compiled an amazing 418–221 record against the nation's best teams.

FULL COURT THREE-ON-THREE DRILL

Dan Miller

Idaho State University

This drill is designed to develop many things in conjunction with defense, namely communication between teammates, stance, one-on-one defense, helping out a beaten teammate, defense away from the ball, footwork, aggressiveness, rebounding, and conditioning. The drill is started by dividing the squad into groups of threes, putting different

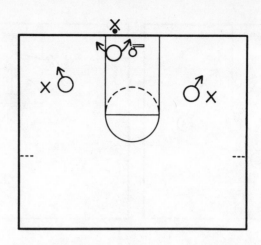

colored shirts on half of them. The ball is inbounded by one group of three while another group picks them up defensively. The first rule of the drill is that the other inbound pass may not be thrown in deeper than the free throw line in the backcourt. This is to prevent the offensive team from throwing a full court pass and defeating the purpose of the drill. The defense tries to prevent the inbound pass and if successful for five seconds, gets the ball on offense. As the ball is inbounded successfully, the defense is talking, switching when necessary, but all the time playing their man as tough as possible. The defense will try to play the man with the ball by means of fronting him and shutting off every move he makes. The other defensive players away from the ball are communicating with the man on the ball, letting him know of any imminent switches or screens and also keeping him aware of where his help is. The three defensive men will have to make all necessary defensive adjustments. Offensively, the three players may do anything they want to bring the ball down the floor and score. The ball is in play until the offense scores or the defense rebounds the ball. In either case, the ball changes hands and the defense inbounds the ball and brings it back down the floor while the team formerly on offense switches to defense.

Dan Miller took over the 1967–68 Idaho State Bengals when Claude Retherford resigned after the first four games, and led them to a third-place finish in the Big Sky Conference and a 13–13 overall season record. That was the first .500 or better finish for Idaho State since the 1962 record of 17–9. Miller had been head freshman coach at ISU and five alums of his frosh team were on the varsity roster.

THREE-ON-THREE FULL COURT DRILL

Ralph Miller

University of Iowa

O=offense. The ball begins out of bounds. The object is to move the ball inbounds, down the court, and score. X=defense. The defense uses full

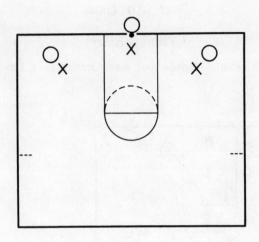

court pressure defense over the entire court. O remains on offense and X on defense until the coach changes the assignment. There are no rules for the offense—they are free-lance. The ball cannot be passed in the air across the mid court line.

Special Value of the Drill

This drill combines every known form and fundamental in the game of basketball. On the full court it puts more pressure upon both units for proper execution because less protection is available. Tough scrimmage conditions of the drill sharpen defensive coverage, backboard screens, ball handling, passing, speed, quickness, and conditioning.

During his four seasons as head basketball coach at the University of Iowa, Ralph Miller's Hawkeyes led the Big Ten in the composite standings with a record of 35 wins and 21 losses for .625. Hawkeye teams coached by Ralph Miller have an overall record of 63 wins and 34 losses for .649. His 1968–69 squad won the co-championship of the Big Ten Conference. Iowa's 10–4 league record and title share in 1968 culminated a steady climb to the top that began in 1965, Miller's first year. Not only have Miller's four Iowa teams established a winning tradition, but 12 of his 13 seasons at his first college post, Wichita State, were winning years also. His overall collegiate record stands at 283 wins, 167 defeats for a .629 percentage. While at Wichita State, he coached three teams which competed in the NIT (1954, 1962, and 1963). Wichita State won the All-College Tournament in Oklahoma City in 1960 and 1963.

Post Cut Drill

Frank Milner
East Orange High School, East Orange, New Jersey

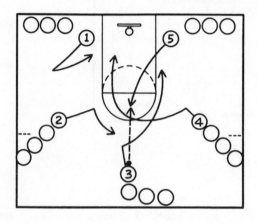

Rotation

1 goes to 2 lane
2 goes to 3 lane
3 goes to 4 lane
4 goes to 5 lane
5 goes to 1 lane

Point man No. 3 passes to pivot lane No. 5, feints left, splits the post as wing man No. 4 feints right, and cuts off the tail of the feeder (feeder goes first). Both cut for goal with pivot passing to either man. The No. 2 wing man also cuts in as *third* cutter and then back for screen shot if neither 3 or 4 is utilized. Pivot man No. 5 also has alternate post man No. 1 who cuts out and back for rebounding as a possible outlet pass. No. 1 rebounds and passes back out to the middle lane. This drill can be changed in many ways (Example: No. 5 post can flash to elbow of the lane and split the post with No. 4 feeding and No. 5 being the second cutter. No. 1 can come around the baseline with No. 2 rebounding.) Other modifications are still possible beyond this.

Special Value of the Drill

The five-man drill is an excellent ball handling drill employing the entire forecourt offensive maneuvering. It is particularly good for teams employing a 1–2–2 or a 3–2 attack. The drill has many uses besides just the splitting of the post which is an early drill of years ago. It may also be used to give a pivot men a chance to pass and cut from outside positions which they seldom have a chance to do. Variations of this drill are numerous, and that is why a drill such as this is so advantageous. It also has triangle rebound potential, as one can readily see from the diagram.

Author of many coaching articles, clinician, District No. 2 Chairman of the High School Division of the National Association of Basketball Coaches, and one of the veteran basketball coaches of the State of New Jersey, Frank Milner has compiled 338 victories against 180 defeats in 26 years of coaching. He began his career at Cliffside Park High School in Cliffside, New Jersey, where, during five seasons, he recorded 85 wins and 15 losses, including two conference, two sectional, and two state championships (1941 and 1948). In 21 years at East Orange High School in East Orange, New Jersey, his record is 253–165. His teams have won three conference, one sectional, and one state championship (1969).

COMBINATION DRILL

Don Morris

East Hardin High School, Glendale, Kentucky

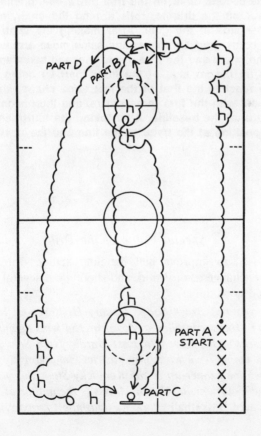

In this drill 12 chairs are placed as follows: three near the sideline, one near the baseline, one at the free-throw line, one at the head of the circle, and the other six in the same arrangement in the other half of the court. The players form a line at the end of the floor opposite the three chairs on the side (part A). The first player dribbles toward the three chairs, using a change of pace until he reaches the first chair. He then fakes to the inside, plants his foot, pushes off in the opposite direction, and goes around the outside of the chair. Immediately upon passing the first chair it is necessary to change direction to the inside of the second chair and also to change hands while dribbling. The dribbler then goes around the third chair in the same manner and continues dribbling down the baseline until he is cut off by the one chair. He then does a reverse pivot with his dribble, rolls around the chair at the baseline, and shoots any one of the following shots: fall away jump shot, regular jump shot after cutting across the lane, regular layup after rolling around the chair, or back-over-the-head layup while going all the way under the goal and shooting on the opposite side. After taking the ball out of the net, he dribbles up the middle of the court (part B) to the first chair at the top of the opposite circle, fakes, plants his foot at one side of the chair, pushes off and changing direction, goes around the chair, immediately encounters the second chair on the free throw line, plants his foot, does a reverse pivot on the dribble, rolls around the chair, and shoots the layup on either side of the goal. After making the shot, he drives the length of the court (part C), makes the same move around the chairs at the head of the circle and the free throw line, and takes another shot. He then dribbles up the far side of the floor (part D) using his change of pace until he reaches the first of the last three chairs, makes the same moves as he did with the first three chairs, and then encounters the last chair of the drill at the baseline. After taking the fourth shot of the drill, he takes his position at the back of the line and the next player begins the drill.

Special Value of the Drill

The drill is used to improve ball handling ability, dribbling, pivoting, change of pace, change of direction, and shooting of several types of shots. It's also a good conditioner.

During seven years at Breckinridge County High School in Hardinsburg, Kentucky, Don Morris compiled a record of 154 wins against 52 losses. In the 1968–69 season he moved to East Hardin High School in Glendale, Kentucky. His teams have won three district championships, two regional championships, one runner-up in the Kentucky State Tournament, and the Kentucky State Tournament. Coach Morris is the author of the book Kentucky High School Basketball *(Parker Publishing Company).*

Attacking Changing Defenses Drill

Gene Paxton

Grand Rapids Junior College

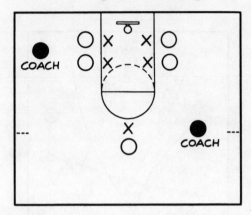

One team on offense is pitted against another team on defense. The offense is run against a variety of defenses (man-to-man, zone, combinations, match-ups, etc) with the defense changing each time the offensive team sets up. One coach is assigned to one team and the other coach to the other. Play may be stopped and corrections made if an error is repeated by either team.

If the offensive team *scores* **they keep possession with an out of bounds play or with a free throw (1+1) situation. On any** *failure* **to score, the fast break is on and it must be defensed by the team formerly on offense. If the team scores on the break they will keep possession and run the set offense.**

Special Value of the Drill

This drill incorporates all the conditions of a game-like scrimmage in a completely controlled situation. It is easy to concentrate on one part while not neglecting the whole situation. It teaches rebounding, passing, dribbling, defense against the break, and the set style of offense against varying defenses.

Coach Gene Paxton joined the staff at Grand Rapids Junior College in 1965 after a highly successful eight-year tenure at Airport Community High School in Carleton, Michigan. In high school he had only one year when a team lost over six games. His teams were noted for their pressure defenses and potent offenses. In his four seasons at Grand Rapids Junior College, his teams have recorded 74 wins against 41 losses. In the 1968–69 season the Raiders posted the most wins ever recorded at Grand Rapids as they finished with a fine 24–9 record. The offensive average during these four years has never fallen below 96 points a game.

FIVE-MAN FUNDAMENTAL DRILL

Dr. Irvin Peterson
Nebraska Wesleyan University

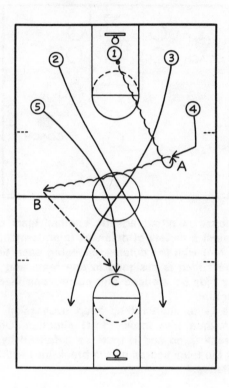

(1) dribbles out to spot A, pivots, and hands off to (4) who dribbles to spot B and then hook passes to (5) who should be at spot C. (2) and (3) are trailers splitting the post. (5) can hand off to either (2) or (3) or fake the ball to them and give the ball to trailer (4). He may also turn and take a jump shot. There are a great many variations that can be used off this basic drill. It may be run with or without a defense.

Special Value of the Drill

In addition to being an excellent conditioning drill, it also gives the players work on ball handling, passing, footwork, and shooting. Fast break responsibilities are emphasized and a coordinated effort is necessary.

The only Nebraska college coach in history ever to win 300 games in his career, Dr. Irvin Peterson has completed 19 seasons at Nebraska Wesleyan

*University. During the 1968–69 campaign his team won 13 games to bring
his overall mark to a lofty 301–170. This feat is even more remarkable
when you consider that Nebraska Wesleyan has no sports grants for its
players. Of 480 coaches in the NCAA basketball guide, Dr. Peterson
ranks No. 20 in the amount of wins, and only nine coaches in the United
States with as many wins have a better percentage than his .639. Seven
Wesleyan teams have been in national tournaments with the 1962 club
(20–8) getting fourth in the NCAA Tournament.*

"CATCH UP" DRILL

Jim Richards

Assistant Coach, Western Kentucky University

**The coach, standing with the ball, calls the name of X1, X2, or X3. The
player whose name is called must touch the baseline in front of him and
then sprint to help his two teammates who have retreated to the opposite
end (in tandem) to prevent the offensive team from scoring on a fast
break. As the coach calls the defensive player's name, he flips the ball**

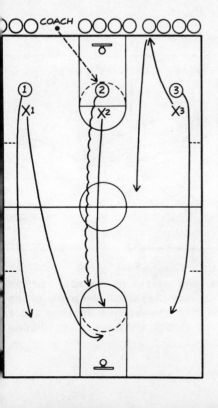
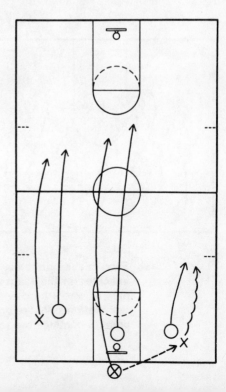

to one of the three offensive players who in turn begin the break (Diagram 1). This makes for a realistic three-on-two fast break with help coming from a late arriving defensive man. When the basket is made by the offensive team or the defensive team rebounds a missed attempt, a man-to-man press is applied by the O's (Diagram 2).

Special Value of the Drill

This drill helps teach the fast break (three-on-two), man-to-man press, offense against the man-to-man press, and reaction from defense to offense. It is a great conditioner. This drill has enough value to warrant its being run almost every day at Western Kentucky University.

During three seasons at Auburn High School in Kentucky, Jim Richards recorded 64 wins against 30 losses and won two district championships. In 1963 he moved to Glasgow High School where, during five seasons, he compiled 112 wins against only 27 losses. His teams at Glasgow won three district, five conference, three regional, and one state championship. In 1968 he became an assistant coach at Western Kentucky University. In his first year his team had a record of 16–10.

DRIBBLE, PIVOT, AND PASS DRILLS

Adolph Rupp
University of Kentucky

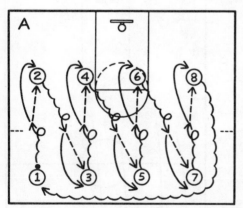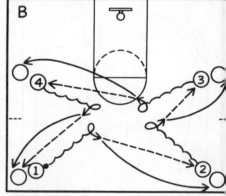

A. Each player dribbles, pivots, and passes to the next man as indicated in the diagram. That man then takes the place of the man to whom he passed. The man who receives the pass at the last station dribbles around the outside and back to the starting point to continue the rotation.

B. Any one of the four players starts the drill by dribbling to the center. When he arrives at the center he stops, pivots, and passes to the next man as shown in the diagram. A defensive player can be added to bother the dribbler. After the dribbler makes his pass, he goes to the end of the line to which he passes.

Kentucky's "Baron of Basketball" is looking for more worlds to conquer, and each step of the way enhances a record of achievement which may never be equalled in the basketball world. A big milestone was reached Jan. 27, 1969, when Coach Rupp recorded his 800th victory as The University of Kentucky coach. During the 1967–68 season, he passed the national record career win mark of 771 set by his old college coach, Forrest (Phog) Allen of Kansas. Rupp's 1967–68 accomplishments, in addition to the record-breaking 772nd victory, included Southeastern Conference Coach of the Year honors after he guided the Wildcats to their 23rd SEC championship. Coach Rupp's list of honors is enormous: election to Naismith Hall of Fame, certification by the NCAA Service Bureau as the nation's most successful collegiate basketball coach, unanimous selection as the national "Coach of the Year" in 1966 for the fourth time in his career, four NCAA Tournament Championships plus all-time record of 16 appearances and more victories (27) in NCAA play than any other coach, a nominal world championship as co-coach of the successful USA entry in the 1948 Olympic Games, election to the Kentucky Hall of Fame, five Sugar Bowl Championships, a NIT title, 16 UK Invitational Tournament trophies, and many, many others.

"BASEBALL" DRILL

Ed Rooney

Grant High School, Portland, Oregon

This is a half court scrimmage. It is used on days before a game and usually lasts for 20 minutes. Three innings are played: the first is man-to-man, the second is zone, and in the third inning, the team decides for itself what defense they will use. Usually the team that wins the flip will take the ball during the last half of the inning. This is an advantage because they know how many runs they need to win. Team A puts the ball in play and does not have to give it up until they have three outs. Outs: any time the other team gets the ball after a bad pass or a rebound, or if the team with the ball commits a turnover, travels, commits an offensive foul, etc. Each basket that is made scores one run and erases all outs. All defensive fouls result in two shots that must be made to erase any previous outs and to score a run.

Special Value of the Drill

This drill comes as close to game conditions as anything we do, unless we are using full court scrimmage to battle for position. In this drill the competition between first and second team has been very fierce, especially after two outs, making the next shot a pressure shot. All free throws have a little pressure on them because a miss on the second shot usually goes to the inside man and is therefore an out. It provides variety and gives the players something they think is different; actually it is not—it's good, hardnose basketball.

Ed Rooney began his coaching career at Jacksonville High School in Jacksonville, Oregon, where, during two seasons, he recorded 40 wins against five losses. In 1954 he moved to St. Helens High School in St. Helens, Oregon. During five seasons there he compiled 109 wins against 21 losses. He attended five state tournaments, winning the State A-2 Championship in 1956. He moved to Grant High School in Portland, Oregon, in 1959. During ten seasons he has compiled a record of 175 wins and 66 losses. His teams have entered the state tournament on five occasions, finishing fifth, third, and, in 1969, winning the State A-1 Championship. His 1968–69 team had a 27–1 record; best ever in the history of A-1 Tournament competition.

Pressure Layup Drill

Paul Stueckler

Robert E. Lee High School, Midland, Texas

On a verbal signal from the coach, O1 will drive toward the basket with his right hand and try to score. X1 will start on the same signal as O1 and will do everything within the rules to keep him from scoring. O1 will then rotate to the line on the left side of the court so that he will have the opportunity to make his initial move toward the basket with his left hand. Everyone must take his turn on both sides of the court on both offense and defense. The coach should be under the basket and stress proper defensive techniques and position from both sides of the basket. It is wise to vary the distance of the starting lines from the basket in order to present different offensive and defensive problems to the boys.

Special Value of the Drill

This drill, which is a great conditioner and excellent for teaching aggressiveness, is one of our favorites because it teaches so many different things

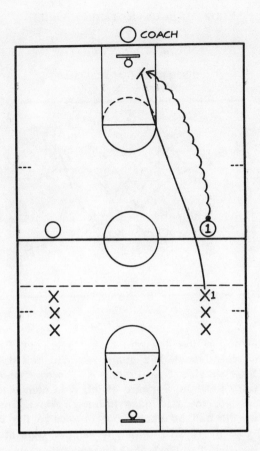

at the same time. It is an exciting drill that contains much game-type action. The drill teaches the following items against game-type pressure:

1. How to drive to the basket from both sides (right and left hands).
2. How to shoot layups and short shots (jumpers and hooks) against defensive pressure from both sides of the basket.
3. How to defend against this type of offensive situation without fouling (we stress baseline position and baseline hand).
4. How to box out in the basket area.

Paul Stueckler has coached high school basketball for 15 years. During that time he has won the championship six times and has been named Coach of the Year in his area on eight occasions. His overall record shows 292 wins and 155 losses. Coach Stueckler spent one year at Presidio, Texas, six years at Austin High School in El Paso, and eight years at Robert E. Lee High School in Midland, Texas. He has coached at Lee since the school opened in 1961.

Four-on-Four Rotation Drill

Phil Vukicevich

University of San Francisco

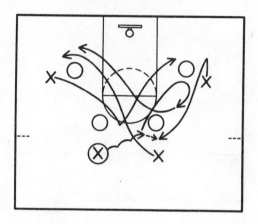

The guard at the top of the key without the ball goes through (skips) and fills at left forward spot. The guard with the ball dribbles toward the forward on the right side. Guard releases to forward and fills the spot at the right forward position. Forward at left side comes to top of key, but instead of getting the ball goes through (skips). The guard who originally handed the ball off comes out to receive the ball but goes through (skips) and guard who originally skipped gets the ball on the next hand off. The order is *release, skip,* and *receive.*

The offense keeps the ball as long as they score or retain possession. A game is ten baskets. Baskets may be subtracted from either team in the event that the coach feels that they failed to be fundamentally sound (e.g., defense failed to screen out, flagrant foul, etc.). As a result, a team which might be ahead can still lose in the event that they get sloppy. Usually two forwards and two guards are used on each team, but post men will be run in the drill to improve their ball handling. The team which loses has to run two full court touch sprints. The competition is very keen and the players work extremely hard to win. An attempt is made to make the teams as even as possible with regard to shooting power, rebounding, etc. The drill is basically like the old figure 8 drill, but four instead of five men are used so that the middle will be kept open. The men are skipped on the rotation to try to eliminate the jump switch. The pattern of movement remains the same as the basic figure 8.

Special Value of the Drill

Offensively, the drill teaches dribbling with the head up and eyes off the floor; how to hand off the ball when moving laterally; individual offensive moves according to how the defense elects to play them; how to pick and roll to the basket; how to go to the offensive basket for tips and rebounds; how to create leads and shake the tight defensive player. It develops better passing; individual shooting proficiency because the drill breaks down to one-on-one moves which are basic to basketball; great team effort in addition to individual effort.

Defensively, the drill teaches sliding through on defense. It develops talk between players; screening out techniques; coordination between players when offensive players release the ball; an understanding of the proper techniques of switching.

Phil Vukicevich began his coaching career as basketball coach and athletic director at San Francisco's Lick-Wilmerding High School. There he guided his team to a Bay Counties League Championship during the second of his two years at Lick. When the USF freshman coaching job fell vacant, he was welcomed back to his alma mater. During a six-year stint at the helm of the Don frosh, he guided the 1962–63 team to a 21–1 mark and the 1964–65 team to a 19–4 record. In two years with the USF varsity he has compiled a 29–22 record.

SITUATION CARDS

Chuck Walker

Assistant Coach, University of Nevada, Reno

30 situations (or any number you desire) are written on 3 x 5 cards which are shuffled and dealt to each squad member. The players are given a few seconds to explain the team solution to each problem situation. The manager then puts the situation on the scoreboard and the ball is put into play.

Examples

1. **We are three points down with one minute left and shooting a one-and-one.**
2. **Five seconds left with a tie score. The ball is out of bounds at mid court.**
3. **Three points ahead with a minute and one half left. We are shooting a one-and-one.**
4. **Taking the "controlled" or strategic foul.**

Special Value of the Drill

1. The drill gives the team confidence in tight situations.
2. It improves team morale (especially during situation practice).
3. Repetition is important in teaching philosophy of handling different situations.

*Currently serving as the assistant basketball coach at the University of Ne-
vada in Reno, Chuck Walker began his coaching career at Placer High
School in Auburn, California, where, over a three-year period, he compiled
a 33–26 record which included a league championship in 1965. In 1966
he moved to Nevada University as the freshman basketball coach. In his
three seasons there he has recorded 40 wins against 16 losses.*

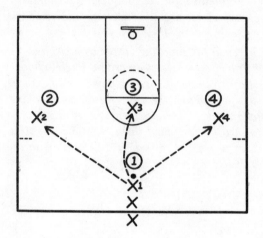

FOUR-ON-FOUR DRILL

Phil Woolpert

University of San Diego

Four-on-Four Drill. X1 may:

1. **Follow pass and screen**
2. **Follow pass and cut for return pass**
3. **Screen away from ball**

**When the play is terminated by a score or by a defensive recovery, two
new men will replace the original passer and his defensive man (X1 and
O1) who in turn replace the original receiver and his defensive man.**

Special Value of the Drill

The drill includes the offensive fundamentals of passing, dribbling, cutting,
screening, pivoting, shooting, rebounding, and meeting the ball. The defensive fundamentals necessary are releasing passer, sloughing, choking
leads, split vision, flexed knees, switching, fighting screens, sliding, playing
dribbler, talking, and blocking out. It is a compact drill which allows controlled supervision, it is competitive, and it requires all the basketball
skills.

Phil Woolpert took over the fading fortunes of the University of San Diego's basketball team in 1962. Prior to this time the Toreros had only one winning season out of six. Since Coach Woolpert's arrival, they have had only one losing campaign out of six, and that was in 1962–63 when he first arrived. His name was known throughout the entire United States as the coach of the great University of San Francisco teams that won two NCAA Championships in 1955 and 1956. He began by handling the University of San Francisco freshman team in 1948 and 1949 along with his high school team. In 1950 Woolpert was selected to guide the destiny of the University of San Francisco, and he stayed there through 1959, compiling 173 wins and 86 defeats. His teams won four West Coast Athletic Conference titles in six years. They won 60 straight games to set a college mark that still stands.